by **Rita Bingham**

With Introduction by **Dr. Lendon Smith, M.D.**

Published by **Natural Meals Publishing**

COUNTRY BEANS introduces the use of bean flours in *CREAM SOUPS, SAUCES, GRAVIES*, as well as added to wheat flour to accomplish protein complimentation, and emphasizes the use of nutritious, basic foods to create fast, low-fat, cholesterol-free meals.

Most COUNTRY BEANS recipes are Gluten-Free and Wheat-Free, suitable for celiacs. See the Gluten-Free Index. Celiacs must be careful to use only approved GF seasonings, mayonnaise, catsup, etc. For more information about Celiac Disease, along with a comprehensive list of foods allowed and foods to avoid, call call (877) CSA-4-CSA, or go online to the Celiac Sprue Association website : http://www.csaceliacs.org.

10th Printing, January, 2005

ISBN 1-882314-11-5
$14.95

Published by *Natural* Meals Publishing
Website : www.naturalmeals.com
E-mail: sales@naturalmeals.com
Order Line: 1.888.232.6706
Printed in United States of America

Cover Photo by Bozarth Photography, Guthrie, OK
Cover design by Rita Bingham
Illustrations by Clair Bingham

COUNTRY BEANS

by Rita Bingham

If you have 30 minutes, you'll have
Great Bean Meals you can eat to your heart's content...
from Family Fare to Classic Cuisine

Dedicated to:

The *Ezra Taft Benson Institute* and the *Agronomy Department* at Brigham Young University, Provo, Utah, for their devotion to people from all over the world in helping them learn to incorporate beans into their diets.

Special thanks to:

My husband, *Clair,* for the "beany" characters in this book, and for his help in testing and developing these good-for-you bean recipes... and for all the meals he cooked so I could have the time to write! (Notice that one "bean guy" is always a bit mischevious!)

Bob's Red Mill, Milwaukie, Oregon, for grinding my bean, pea and lentil flours and marketing them throughout the US and Canada.

K-TEC of Orem, Utah, for the wide variety of beans used in the cover photo of this book

Introduction by
Dr. Lendon H. Smith, M.D.

I have been giving advice about diet, vitamins and nutrition for more than 15 years, believing that good nutrition is the basis for overcoming illness. Today's parents of small children grew up believing that good nutrition could be purchased in a box or a can. The health problems children of today are facing are prompting parents to carefully analyze the foods they serve.

The new U.S. Department of Agriculture dietary guideline using the Eating Right Pyramid is right in line with what I've been recommending for years! The USDA now suggest that the foods *lowest* in fats, oils and sugars (fruits, vegetables, dry beans and grains) should make up the largest portion of our daily meals.

Eliminating, or drastically reducing meat and dairy products creates a large void in the diet of most Americans. The information contained in this book will make it easy to fill that void. The benefits of using beans on a daily basis have recently been promoted because studies show beans help to reduce cholesterol while providing excellent nutrition. When combined with nuts, seeds or grains, they form a complete high-fiber vegetable protein. A three-ounce steak will provide 350 calories and only about 15 grams of usable protein. One and one-fourth cups of cooked beans will provide the same number of calories and yet deliver 50% *more* usable protein. And, since beans are only 2-3% fat, you have a virtually fat-free source of protein, with NO cholesterol.

But who wants to sit down to one and one-fourth cups of cooked beans every day? And who wants to spend hours cooking beans every day? With the ingenious (and sometimes down-right sneaky) techniques set forth in this book, you can use beans in one form or another in almost everything you serve and still make a meal in 30 minutes or less.

By using beans ground to a flour in all your baked goods, you not only create a perfect protein, you also add valuable B vitamins, carbohydrates and iron. Creamy soups, sauces and gravies to rival canned or packaged brands are thickened with bean flour and are made without any fat or dairy products. Busy cooks will be happy to know that these soups and sauces cook in only 3 minutes. They're almost instant, and much *more* nutritious and much *less* expensive than those available from the supermarket.

The recipes found in Country Beans will make it easy for you to get back to basics *fast*, which is the way most of our meals need to be prepared these days. So let's get cooking with beans and start eating right!

Lendon H. Smith

Table of Contents

Basic Ingredients Used In This Book....5
Equipment and Supplies To Have On Hand....6
Better Breakfasts....7
Breakfast Drinks and Shakes....10
Breakfasts Breads & Muffins....12
Quick Breads....18
Yeast Breads....24
Dressings....30
Salads....33
Dips & Sandwich Fillings....51
Sauces & Gravies....58
Toppings & Coatings....62
Seasonings....64
Patties....68
Loaves....74
Hearty Bean Soups....78
Casseroles & One-Dish Meals....100
Side Dishes....119
Company Dinners....124
Snacks....131
Cookies & Bars....134
Puddings, Pies, Cakes....143
Candies using Tofu and Okara....149
Tofu and Okara (Making)....151
Cooking Options....154
Cooking Cracked Beans....155
Instant Mashed Beans....155
Gluten-Free Baked Goods....156
Home Canning....157
Information Section....164
Grinding Beans to a Flour....174
Buying and Storing Beans....175
Sprouting Dry Beans....177
Preparing beans for Use in Recipes....178
Soaking & Cooking Beans....179
Cooking Bean Flour....180
Publications to Order....183
Sources for Equipment and Supplies....183, 184
INDEX (GLUTEN-FREE RECIPES MARKED "GF")....185
INDEX TO BEAN FLOUR RECIPES....194

About the Author
and the *Natural* Meals In Minutes style of eating

Since 1966, Rita Bingham has encouraged healthy eating, carrying on the tradition of her mother, Esther Dickey who over 30 years ago wrote **Passport to Survival** (a comprehensive guide to using and storing basic foods). Rita uses those nutritious foods to create fast recipes for every meal of the day, even snacks and desserts! Her husband and 5 children, as well as thousands of seminar participants, have given Rita's recipes rave reviews!

The *NATURAL* MEALS IN MINUTES and COUNTRY BEANS cookbooks cover the use of a wide variety of grains, seeds and beans to make hundreds of delicious, low-fat, well balanced vegetarian meals in 30 minutes or less.

Whole grains can be cracked or ground to a fine flour to reduce cooking time. They provide the basis for hundreds of delicious patties, cereals, breads, soups, salads, sandwich fillings, casseroles and even desserts.

Sprouts provide a fresh, high quality source of vitamin C as well as many other nutrients. Rita gives several fail-proof methods as well as recipes calling for sprouts at every meal of the day.

Also included are easy to follow instructions on how to use powdered milk to make non-fat cheeses, buttermilk, yogurt and yogurt cheeses, along with recipes which call for those cheeses.

Beans ground to a flour cook in only 3 minutes to make fat-free creamy soups, sauces and gravies you can eat to your heart's content. Time saving advance preparation techniques will help you make these *fast* bean recipes in a flash!

You will be amazed at the hundreds of new, heart-healthy ways to use beans.

BEAN FLOURS – FOR *FAST,* HEALTHY MEALS

We all know how long it CAN take to cook beans, but they can now be served as *fast foods* with this breakthrough for the 90's. *Revolutionary* NEW *bean soups, from first step to first bite in 3 minutes or less, complete bean meals in 30 minutes or less,* using bean flours and pre-cooked beans (canned, bottled or frozen).

So, bring those beans out of the pantry and give them the place on your table they deserve! *Make them the main attraction with these simple, new ideas.*

This book will teach you to use DRY BEANS in the following ways:

- as a FINE BEAN FLOUR, purchased or ground at home
- sprouted to be eaten raw, lightly steamed, or cooked
- cooked using either the quick-soak or overnight soak methods
- pressure cooked or pressure bottled as whole beans or bean soups
- cooked, cooled and refrigerated for up to 5 days or frozen
- cracked, using a blender, seed or grain grinder

In this book, nearly 120 recipes call for **bean flour** because this is the fastest and most nutritious way to cook beans. Bean flour can be ground at home using an electric or hand grinder, or can be *purchased* from BOB'S RED MILL, 5209 S. E. INTERNATIONAL WAY, MILWAUKIE, OR 97222, (503) 654-3215. The Red Mill products are available in health stores and supermarkets across the U.S., especially on the West Coast. Call for a catalog or for a retailer near you. Flours available are: White Bean, Black Bean, Pinto Bean, Garbanzo Bean, Green Pea, and Red Lentil.

For "How To" Information on Grinding Bean Flours, see p. 174; Sprouting, see p. 177; Cooking with bean flours, see pages 4, 6, 155, 156, 172, 180. For sources of equipment, supplies and basic foods, see pp. 183, 184.

Baby lima and small white beans are my favorite because they can be used to make great cream sauces and soups which are gluten-free, wheat-free, fat-free and dairy-free. Also, they can be added to any recipe calling for wheat flour to achieve protein complimentation and to add additional fiber and essential nutrients. These beans could be substituted for the beans listed in almost any recipe in this book. Other favorites are pinto, small red and garbanzo.

COMPARE THE COST

When served as a source of protein, beans cost less than 10¢ per serving, compared to commercial cheeses at 40¢ per serving and meats at 75¢ per serving!

COOKING BEAN FLOUR

No more soaking, boiling, simmering, waiting or mashing!

Soups, Sauces, Gravies, Thickeners Beans ground to a fine flour can be mixed with cool water and then whisked into boiling water and seasonings to make an *almost instant soup or thickener* in only 3 minutes... (learn how in the Hearty Bean Soups Section); refried beans in only 5 minutes for bean-filled burritos- from dry bean flour to first tasty bite- in only minutes! See page 155 to make "Instant Mashed Beans" which can be used in any recipe calling for cooked mashed beans, including sandwich fillings and dips.

Bean flour combined with wheat flour accomplishes protein complimentation. This is an excellent way to increase the protein in your meals and to introduce beans slowly into the diet. Bean flour can be used in any recipe calling for flour by *replacing up to 25% of the wheat flour with any variety of bean flour.* (I most often use lima or small white beans because they are the mildest in flavor and lightest in color.) If the recipe calls for 2 c. flour, you could add up to 1/2 c. bean flour. I usually add an extra egg or other leavening, such as 1 t. white vinegar.

COUNTRY BEANS UNLOCKS THE MYSTERY OF HOW TO MAKE BEANS "USER FRIENDLY"!

When we eat too many refined foods, our bodies no longer have the enzymes to properly digest high in fiber beans and grains. Using one or all of the following tips will help you overcome that four letter word — *GASS!* (**See Information Section for more details.**)

- Use sprouted beans, as the sprouting process develops enzymes to help digest beans more easily.
- Soak beans using the overnight or quick soak method (see p. 178), then discard soaking water. Add fresh water to cook beans. This process is more helpful than adding soda, ginger, or other spices to eliminate gas.
- Start with small amounts of beans or bean flour several times weekly in soups, sauces, all baked goods, to help get used to them slowly (but surely!).

NUTRITIONAL ADVANTAGES OF BEANS

Most beans contain only 2-3% fat. You may never have to count calories again! Beans are the perfect food for fat-restricted diets!

Got High Cholesterol? Beans are cholesterol-free and full of SOLUBLE FIBER. One of the BEST ways to lower your cholesterol levels is to eat more BEANS!!!

High in Protein, Carbohydrates, B Vitamins and Iron. Most beans contain at least 20% protein and are high in carbohydrates which provide long-lasting energy. In addition. beans provide essential B Vitamins and Iron. Adding beans to your daily meals insures total nutrition!

BASIC INGREDIENTS:

Vegetable- or Meat-based Bouillons and Soup Bases for Seasoning. Look for those low in salt and without MSG.

Salt-Free Seasonings available from your grocery or health food store. Made with herbs, spices and often sesame seeds. Also, see the COUNTRY BEANS Seasoning Section. (Excellent for seasoning cooked vegetables, patties, loaves and soups)

Herbs and Spices for seasoning

Flavorings - Soy sauce, Worcestershire sauce, Sesame Oil (Flavored) - available in Oriental section of grocery store

Sweeteners - Honey is used almost exclusively. Where powdered sugar is called for, I generally use powdered Sucanat (dried cane juice). See instructions in Cooking Options Section, p. 156).

Grains - Wheat, Rice, Barley, Oats - Whole, Cracked, Rolled and as a Flour

Beans - Whole, Cracked, Ground to a Flour, Raw, Bottled, Canned, Cooked, Sprouted, Frozen
Varieties: Black, Blackeye Peas, Garbanzo, Great Northern, Kidney, Lima, Mung, Navy, Pea, Pinto, Red, Pink, Soy, Green and Yellow Whole and Split Peas, Red and Green Lentils

Dry Milk Powder (less expensive and tastier than "grocery store variety" instant powder, and it stores longer) Note: Powdered Instant milk from Food Storage Supplier or Health Stores tastes great and stores well.

For WHEAT-FREE, GLUTEN-FREE baking, wheat flour is replaced with a combination of white or brown rice flour, corn flour, xanthan gum, potato starch flour, and tapioca flour. See next page for GF (Gluten Free) baking mix formula. Celiacs must also be careful to use GF soy sauce, bouillons, and other seasonings called for in these recipes.

EQUIPMENT AND SUPPLIES TO HAVE ON HAND

Cast iron or heavy skillet

Hand or electric grain grinder/cracker (See page183 for sources.)
K-Tec Kitchen Mill and the GrainMaster Whisper Mill are guaranteed to grind all types of beans and grains.
Sturdy hand mill or electric seed or coffee mill to grind smaller quantities of beans or grains from coarse crack to fine flour.

Hand food grinder or food processor

Heavy duty blender

Quart jars with sieve lids or sprouting trays

Colander

Large strainer

Wire whisk

Graters - large, medium and small

Muffin tins

Baking trays

Heavy saucepans with tight-fitting lids (stainless steel or cast iron are best)

Assorted casserole/cake pans

Non-stick cooking spray

Pressure cooker/canner (optional, but very helpful)

Cheesecloth or loose-weave fabric to make tofu

RITA'S GLUTEN FREE BAKING MIX

(If you have wheat or gluten allergies, use this mix in place of the flours called for in the breads, cakes, cookies and some cereals in this book. Adding extra protein in the form of eggs helps produce a lighter product.) Check your health food store for these products.

Other excellent gluten-free flours are lentil, pea, amaranth, and quinoa.

3 c. brown rice flour
1 c. tapioca flour
2/3 c. corn flour
1 T. xanthan gum
2 c. potato starch flour
1/2 c. soy or garbanzo bean flour
1/2 c. buckwheat flour
(to give the flour a "brown" color)

BETTER BREAKFASTS

Start your day right with a stick-to-the-ribs breakfast of whole grains and nutritious beans to help avoid the 10:00 a.m. urge to snack on not-so-healthful foods.

See page 6 for the Gluten-Free flour mixture to replace the wheat flour called for in this section.

SPICY HONEY NUTS

2 1/2 c. whole wheat flour
1/2 c. white bean flour
1/2 c. dry milk powder
1/2 c. brown sugar (opt.)
1/2 t. salt
1/4 t. ea. ginger and cinnamon
1/4 c. melted honey
2 t. pure vanilla extract
approx. 6 T. water

Mix dry ingredients. Using electric mixer or rotary egg beater, drizzle in honey and vanilla and only enough water to make a fine, crumbly mixture. DO NOT make a dough.

Note: Because moisture content of flours vary, the amount of water used will differ. The mixture should be similar in size and texture to dry commercial Grape Nuts.

Spread evenly on a large baking sheet and bake at 325° for 10 minutes. Stir to break up granules and bake 5-10 minutes longer, or until golden brown. Allow to cool and serve with milk or store in air-tight container.

MOIST NUT 'N HONEY GRANOLA

2 c. sunflower seeds
1 c. sesame seeds
1 c. whole wheat flour
1/2 c. soy or white bean flour
10 c. rolled oats
3 c. chopped almonds (optional)
2 c. shredded coconut
1 t. salt
2 t. cinnamon
2 c. honey or part brown sugar
1/4 c. molasses
1 c. water
2 T. vanilla

Put all dry ingredients in a bowl and mix well. Combine all moist ingredients and heat to melt honey. Pour over dry ingredients and mix well. Spread thin on baking sheets and bake at 325° for 20-30 minutes, stirring every 5 minutes to break up chunks. Reduce heat to 250° and bake an additional 30 minutes, stirring occasionally.

Allow to cool and add raisins or other dried fruits, if desired. Store in air-tight container. Makes one gallon.

HI-PRO CEREAL MIX

3/4 c. whole wheat
1/2 c. brown rice
1/4 c. flax seed
1/4 c. sesame seeds
1/2 c. almonds
1 c. rolled oats
1/4 c. oat bran
1/4 c. corn meal
2 T. coarse garbanzo bean flour
1/2 t. ginger
1 c. shredded coconut
4 t. salt (opt.)
dried fruit bits

In seed mill or blender, crack wheat, brown rice and seeds (one kind at a time) to the consistency of corn meal. Combine with remaining ingredients. Cover and store in refrigerator.

To cook, mix 2 c. water with 1 c. cereal mix. Bring to a full boil, then cover and remove from heat. Let sit 15 minutes. Or, for a "mushier" cereal, add only 1/2 c. mixture, bring to a boil and simmer 15 minutes. Serve with honey and butter.

WHEAT, BEANS & RICE CEREAL

1/2 cup each coarsely ground white bean flour, wheat flour, brown rice flour
(The texture should be coarse, like commercial cream of wheat.)

Add 1/2 c. mix to 2 c. warm water and 1/2 t. salt. Bring to a boil. Reduce heat to low, cover pan and cook 5 minutes, stirring occasionally. Serve with milk and honey and a little vanilla.

BREAKFAST PITA PIZZAS

4 eggs
1/3 c. water
2 T. dry milk powder
1 T. vegetable soup base
2 T. Picante sauce

• • •

4 whole pitas or flour tortillas
2 c. grated Mozzarella cheese
2 c. cooked garbanzo beans
2 T. chopped ripe olives (opt.)

Preheat oven to 350°. Blend eggs, water, milk powder, base and Picante sauce, pour into skillet that has been coated with cooking spray and scramble until barely cooked. Place pitas on large baking sheet and top each with 1/4 of scrambled egg mixture, beans, cheese and olives.

Bake or broil until cheese bubbles (about 8 minutes). Serve whole or slice each pizza into wedges and serve as appetizers. Serves 4-6.

BREAKFAST DRINKS AND SHAKES

Instant nutrition in a glass! Breakfasts don't have to be hot to be filling and good for you. These drinks — high in protein, brimming with high energy and fruit juice— are sure to please teenagers on the go. Great for snacks too! For a delicious low-fat ice cream, freeze mixture, then process through a Champion Juicer, heavy duty blender or food processor.

These recipes call for Tofu which may be purchased, or see the section on homemade Tofu and Okara (the by-product of Tofu).

All recipes in this section are Gluten-Free.

CREAMY BANANA-BERRY DRINK

1/2 c. tofu
1/2 c. frozen blackberries
1 t. vanilla
1 frozen banana
1/3 c. frozen apple juice concentrate
up to 1/4 c. cold water

Blend all ingredients until smooth, adding only enough water to make a thick shake. Serves 2.

RASPBERRY FREEZE

1/2 c. tofu
1 c. frozen raspberries
1 t. vanilla
1 frozen banana
3/4 c. frozen apple juice concentrate
up to 2 c. cold water

Blend all ingredients, adding only enough water to make a thick shake. Serves 2.

TOFU EGGNOG

1 egg
*6 T. tofu powder**
dash salt
pinch nutmeg
1 c. ice water
1 T. light honey
1/4 t. vanilla
1/8 t. rum flavoring

*"Better Than Milk" is made from tofu and is sold in powdered form in many health stores. Blend all ingredients. Serves 2.

MANDARIN TANGERINE FREEZE

1 frozen banana
*6 T. tofu powder**
1/2 c. cold water
1 c. frozen Dole Mandarin Tangerine juice concentrate
1/2 t. vanilla

*"Better Than Milk" is made from tofu and is sold in powdered form in many health stores. Blend all ingredients. Serves 2.

BREAKFAST BREADS AND MUFFINS

The combination of beans and grains forms a perfect protein, and using bean flour in breads provides an easy way to "hide" beans, for those of us who have skeptical or picky eaters! Beans can be added whole, mashed, (see Cooking Options Section for "Instant Mashed Beans"), in the form of Okara or as a flour to easily and quickly make naturally nutritious, complete protein whole grain breads and muffins.

**Starred bean ingredients are those which may need some explanation. Please refer to the Cooking Options Section for an explanation or for substitution.*

See Page 6 for the Gluten-Free flour mix to replace the wheat called for in these recipes.

MAMA'S MAGIC MUFFIN MIX

LeArta Moulton (author of The Amazing Wheat Book) is the creator of this mix that is so versatile it's magic! Makes muffins, waffles, cakes, cupcakes, cookies, etc. all with *one* batter.

Place in bowl and set aside: ***2 c. boiling water*** and ***2 c. flaked bran***. Beat together ***1/2 c. oil or applesauce, 2 c. honey*** (or white sugar, brown sugar, date sugar) and ***4 eggs***. Add ***2 c. buttermilk, 1 t. salt, 5 t. soda, 5 t. vanilla, 4 1/2 c. whole wheat flour, 1/2 c. white bean flour*** and ***cooled bran mixture.***

Mix well. Can be stored in an air-tight container and kept in refrigerator up to 1 month. (Add extra water or flour if your refrigerated batter becomes too thick or too thin.) Use to make one of the following:

MOIST MUFFINS - To 3 c. of basic batter, bake as is or add 1/2 c. chopped dates, nuts, raisins, blueberries. Fill muffin tins (coated with cooking spray) 3/4 full. Bake at 375° for 20 min.

NUTTY BANANA BREAD To 3 c. basic batter, add 2 t. vanilla, 2 mashed ripe bananas, 1 c. chopped nuts, 1/2 t. ea. cinnamon and cloves. Bake in loaf pan coated with cooking spray, or 9" square cake pan. 50-60 min. at 350°.

TRIPLE DUTY GF MUFFIN MIX

2 c. brown rice flour
1/2 c. potato starch flour
1/2 c. tapioca flour
1/4 c. white or pinto bean flour
1 t. baking soda
1 T. Egg Replacer
1 t. xanthan gum
1/3 cup Sucanat or powdered honey
2 t. dried lemon peel or powdered vanilla
1 t. salt

Mix together all the ingredients and store in an airtight container. Makes enough for 4 batches of baking.

Triple Duty Mix adapted from recipe by Bette Hagman, "More From the Gluten-Free Gourmet", Henry Holt & Co, 1993.

MUFFINS - To 1 cup of mix, beat together 2 eggs, 2 T. canola oil or applesauce, 1/3 c. buttermilk or fruit juice. Pour into the flour mix and beat until smooth. Do not over-beat. Spoon into 6 muffin cups coated with cooking spray and bake at 375° for 12-15 minutes. Makes 6. TO VARY TASTE: Add 1/4 c. raisins, nuts, mashed bananas or chopped dates.

CAKE - Mix as for muffins but add 1 more T. Sucanat to 1 c. mix and spoon dough into a greased 8" round cake pan. Bake at 350° for 20-25 minutes. Serve with whipped cream and fruit, or frost to your taste.

CRANBERRY ORANGE BREAKFAST SQUARES

1 1/2 c. whole wheat flour
1/2 c. white bean flour
1 1/2 t. baking powder
1/2 t. salt
1/4 c. dry milk powder
1 T. frozen orange juice concentrate
3/4 c. warm water
3/4 c. honey
1 egg
1 c. chopped nuts
1 c. whole, raw cranberries, blueberries or finely grated apples

Mix moist and dry ingredients separately. Stir liquid ingredients into the dry mixture. Stir in nuts and berries. Spread into 9"x13" baking pan that has been coated with cooking spray and place in 350° oven. Bake 20-25 minutes, or until cake tests done. Cut into squares and serve with honey or honey butter. OR, sprinkle with topping before baking.

Topping:
*2 c. quick oats or dry Okara**
1/4 c. white bean flour
1 c. shredded coconut
4 T. melted honey
3 T. butter (opt.)

* See Tofu and Okara Section.

With hand or electric mixer, mix all ingredients together. Sprinkle over unbaked cake.

HIGH PROTEIN APPLEJACKS

3 c. whole wheat flour
1 c. fine white bean flour
1 T. baking soda
1/2 c. dry milk powder or whey
1/2 t. salt
2 T. honey
2 c. buttermilk
2 c. warm water
3 T. canola oil or applesauce
4 egg yolks
4 beaten egg whites
1 lg. grated apple

Combine ingredients in order given. This recipe can be used to make waffles, hot cakes or Ebelskivers. Serves 4-6. Note: For extra crunch, add 1/4 c. chopped nuts or sunflower seeds to batter.

PERFECT BUTTERMILK PANCAKES
Wheat and Gluten Free

1/3 c. tapioca flour
2/3 c. brown rice flour
1/3 c. white bean flour
1 t. baking powder
1/2 t. baking soda
1/2 t. salt
2 T. canola oil or applesauce
1 T. honey
2 eggs, separated (whites beaten stiff)
3/4 c. fresh buttermilk

Mix ingredients in order given, folding in egg whites last. Pour 2" circles of batter onto griddle coated with cooking spray, on medium heat. These require longer, slower cooking than wheat pancakes. Cook until golden brown.

PERFECT PANCAKES Gluten-Lactose Free

1/3 c. tapioca flour
2/3 c. brown rice flour
1/3 c. white bean flour
2 T. honey
1 1/2 t. baking powder
1/2 t. salt
2 eggs, separated (whites beaten stiff)
1 c. water
2 T. canola oil or applesauce
1/4 t. vanilla (opt.)
pinch of allspice or ginger (opt.)

Mix ingredients in order given, folding in egg whites last. Pour 2" circles of batter onto griddle coated with cooking spray. These require longer, slower cooking than wheat pancakes. Cook until golden brown on both sides.

NUT 'N HONEY BRAN MUFFINS

1 c. boiling water
3 t. baking soda
2 1/2 c. flaked bran
1 c. honey
1/4 c. canola oil or applesauce
3 eggs
1 T. vanilla
2 1/2 c. yogurt
2 t. cinnamon
1/2 c. oatmeal
1/2 t. salt
1/2 c. white bean flour
2 c. whole wheat flour
1 c. raisins or chopped fruit
1 c. chopped nuts - topping

Put soda in boiling water and pour over bran. Add honey, oil or applesauce, vanilla and eggs. Stir well. Add remaining ingredients, except nuts, and mix well. Fill muffin tins that have been coated with cooking spray 3/4 full and top with nuts. Bake at 400° for 15-20 minutes. For **6-Week Refrigerator Muffins,** double this recipe and store batter in covered container for up to 6 weeks, using only as much as needed, then returning remainder to fridge. Add chopped nuts to tops of muffins before baking.

GREAT WHEAT MUFFINS

1 3/4 c. whole wheat flour
1/4 c. pinto bean flour
3 t. baking powder
1 t. salt
3 T. molasses or honey
3/4 c. chopped dates
1 c. chopped nuts
1 c. milk
1 egg
1/4 c. canola oil or applesauce

Combine dry ingredients. Add remaining ingredients and stir just until mixed. Fill muffin tins that have been coated with cooking spray 3/4 full. Bake about 20 minutes at 425°, until delicately browned.

THE MUFFIN BAR

(A fun way to please a variety of tastes.)

1 T. baking powder
*1 c. wheat germ or Okara**
2 c. water
1 T. vanilla
2 3/4 c. whole wheat flour
1/4 c. white bean flour
1/3 c. honey
1/2 c. canola oil or applesauce

* See Tofu and Okara Section.

Mix with **ONE** of the following:

1/4 c. jelly or jam
(1 t. in center of each muffin)
1/2 c. peanut butter mixed with 2/3 c. honey
1 c. fresh or frozen blueberries
1/2 c. chopped green onions
1 c. raisins
1 c. chopped nuts
1/4 c. chopped green chiles
1/4 c. Picante Sauce
1 c. grated cheese

Coat large muffin tins with cooking spray. Mix dry ingredients and flavor with one of the above ingredients. OR, fill muffin tins 1/2 full and let the "eaters" choose from a display of optional ingredients. Stir about 1 t. into each muffin. Top with remaining batter (fill 3/4 full) and bake at 425° 17-20 minutes or until golden brown. Makes 10-12 muffins.

CINNAMON-APPLE MUFFINS

1 c. whole wheat flour
1/3 c. white bean flour
1/2 c. flaked bran
2 T. dry milk powder
1 t. baking powder
1/2 t. baking soda
1/4 t. salt
1/4 t. cinnamon
pinch nutmeg
1 c. raisins
1 c. walnuts, chopped
1 c. grated apple
1/3 c. canola oil or applesauce
2 eggs, beaten
2/3 c. water
2/3 c. melted honey

Thoroughly mix dry ingredients. Make a nest in the dry mixture and add moist ingredients, stirring only enough to blend.

Fill muffin tins that have been coated with cooking spray 3/4 full. Bake at 375° for 25 to 30 minutes. Serve hot.

SPICY OATMEAL MUFFINS

1 c. oatmeal
1 c. warm water
*3/4 c. mashed pinto beans**
2 egg whites
1 egg
1/4 c. melted butter or applesauce
1 c. honey
2 1/4 c. whole wheat flour
2 T. dry milk powder
1 T. baking powder
1/4 t. salt
1 t. cinnamon
1/4 t. nutmeg
1 c. chopped walnuts
1/2 c. raisins

*See Cooking Options section for "Instant Mashed Beans."

In a large bowl, mix oats and warm water. Let stand 3 minutes. Meanwhile, measure and mix dry ingredients. Beat liquids into oat mixture until smooth. Add nuts, raisins and mixed dry ingredients and stir just until moistened.

Fill muffin tins coated with cooking spray 3/4 full OR pour into 9"x13" or larger pan. Bake at 350° for 20-25 minutes, or until a toothpick inserted in center comes out clean. Let cool 5 minutes before removing from pan.

QUICK BREADS

These whole grain breads, with the addition of bean flour, provide a complete protein. . .perfect for any meal of the day! ***See Cooking Options Section for information on grinding beans to a fine flour.***

See Page 6 for a Gluten-Free mix to use in these recipes in place of wheat flour.

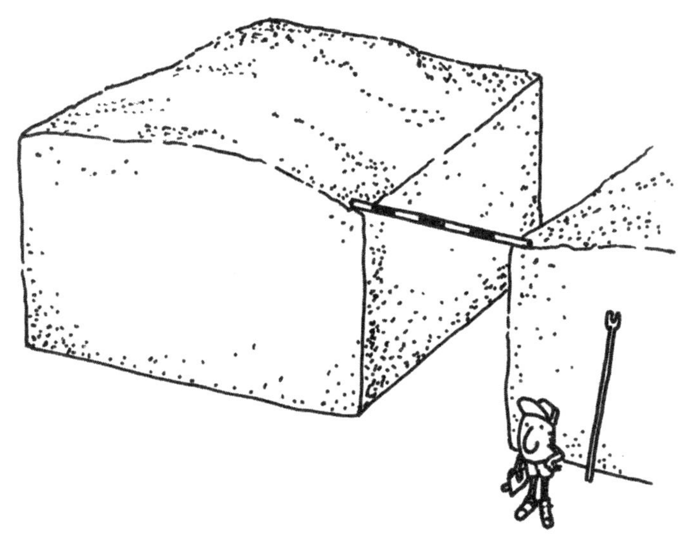

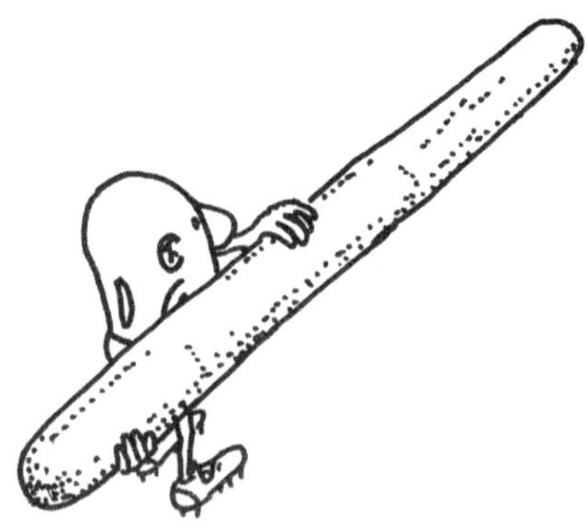

SESAME CORN BREAD

3/4 c. whole wheat flour
1/4 c. fine pea flour
1/2 c. honey
1 1/2 t. salt
1 1/4 t. soda
2 c. cornmeal
1 c. oat bran
1/2 c. sesame seeds, toasted
1/3 c. canola oil or applesauce
*1/2 t. flavored sesame oil**
2 eggs, slightly beaten
2 c. buttermilk

Mix dry ingredients. In a separate bowl, mix moist ingredients. Combine and mix just until dry ingredients are moistened. Pour into muffin tins that have been coated with cooking spray, filling nearly to top. *Found in oriental section of grocery store.

Bake at 375° for 25-30 minutes. Serve hot or cold.

CORN DODGERS

1 c. corn meal
2 T. pea flour
1 t. salt, chicken or vegetable soup base
1 T. canola oil or applesauce
1 1/2 t. honey
1 c. boiling water

Combine dry ingredients. Add honey to water and pour over dry ingredients. Beat until well blended. Drop the batter from a tablespoon onto a baking sheet that has been coated with cooking spray.

Bake about 20 minutes. Makes 12 dodgers. OR, drop into a hot skillet that has been coated with cooking spray and brown on both sides.

QUICK AND EASY CORN BREAD SQUARES

3/4 c. fine corn meal or corn flour
2 T. whole wheat flour
2 T. pea flour
2 t. baking powder
2 T. dry milk powder
1/4 t. salt
1 T. honey
1 egg
3 T. canola oil or applesauce
1/2 c. warm water

Combine dry ingredients. Combine moist ingredients and mix into dry mixture, just until dry ingredients are moistened. Pour into 9"x13" pan that has been coated with cooking spray.

Bake at 425° about 15 minutes, or until golden brown.

TOFU-SESAME BREAD STICKS

Blend until smooth:
2 c. tofu
1/3 c. canola oil or applesauce
1 1/2 t. chicken or vegetable soup base
2 1/2 t. baking powder

Pour into mixing bowl. Using an electric mixer, beat in:
1/2 c. sesame seeds
1/2 t. parsley flakes
2 1/4 c. whole wheat flour
1/4 c. lentil flour

Beat dough for 1-2 minutes, until it becomes elastic and smooth. Roll into a long snake and cut in 1" sections. Roll each into thin sticks. Place 1" apart on baking sheets that have been coated with cooking spray.

Bake at 375° for 20-30 minutes or until golden brown. Serve warm or cool.

Option: Mix 1/3 c. fat-free mayonnaise, 1/3 c. parmesan cheese and 2 T. sesame seeds. Roll unbaked sticks to coat. Proceed as above.

BOB'S BEST BISCUITS (GLUTEN-FREE)

(Great Tasting, Light and Fluffy)

*2 c. Rita's Gluten-Free flour**
1 1/2 t. xanthan gum
3/4 t. salt
4 t. baking powder
1 t. warmed honey
2 T. canola oil or applesauce
1 egg
3/4 c. warm water

Mix dry ingredients together, then add moist ingredients and stir well for 30 seconds.

Pat out the mixture to 1" thick on lightly floured board and cut into square or round biscuits. Or, make drop biscuits by dropping the batter by tablespoonfuls onto a baking sheet coated with cooking spray.

Bake on a baking sheet coated with cooking spray at 425° for 15 minutes. Makes 8 2" biscuits.

*If desired, 2 c. whole wheat flour can be substituted for the GF flour (see recipe on p. 6) and the xanthan gum..

BEAN 'N NUT BREAD

1/2 c. honey
1/4 c. canola oil or applesauce
1 c. mashed beans- any kind*
1/2 c. warm water
1 egg
2 c. whole wheat flour
1/2 t. cinnamon
1/4 t. nutmeg
1/2 t. salt
2 t. baking powder
1 c. chopped nuts

*See Cooking Options Section for "Instant Mashed Beans."

Mix and add ingredients in order given.

Put in loaf pan that has been coated with cooking spray and bake 45 minutes at 350° OR fill 10-12 muffin tins and bake for 20-25 minutes.

OATMEAL DATE AND NUT BREAD

2 c. boiling water
1 c. rolled oats
1/2 c. honey
2 t. salt
1 T. canola oil or applesauce
1 T. active dry yeast
1/2 c. lukewarm water
2/3 c. each chopped nuts and dates
3/4 c. white bean flour
4 1/4 c. whole wheat flour

Pour boiling water over oatmeal and let stand until cool. Combine yeast, water and a little of the honey and let rise double (about 10 minutes). Add to cooled oat mixture along with honey, salt and oil. Add nuts, dates and flour; mix thoroughly.

Let rise double (this step can be omitted), then shape into 2 loaves. Place shaped loaves in loaf pans that have been coated with cooking spray and let rise in a warm place until double.

Bake at 400° 20 minutes, then 350° for 40 minutes, until tops are delicately browned.

BANANA NUT BREAD

1 1/2 c. whole wheat flour
1/2 c. blackeye or green pea flour
1/2 t. baking powder
1/2 t. baking soda
1 t. salt
1 T. dry milk powder
1/4 c. canola oil or applesauce
1 c. chopped nuts
2/3 c. mashed ripe bananas
1 egg
3 T. water
1/2 t. lemon juice
1/2-3/4 c. honey

Combine dry ingredients. Cream oil or applesauce, egg and honey and beat thoroughly. Add mashed bananas; mix with remaining ingredients and add to dry mixture, stirring until just moistened.

Pour into loaf pan that has been coated with cooking spray and bake 50-60 minutes at 350°.

Option: Spoon into a 9"x13" pan or muffin tins and bake 20-25 minutes at 375°.

TENDER ZUCCHINI BREAD

2 c. whole wheat flour
1/2 c. white bean flour
1/2 t. salt
1 t. baking soda
2 t. cinnamon
1 egg and 3 egg whites
1/2 c. melted honey
1 t. vanilla
2 c. finely grated zucchini
1/4 c. canola oil or applesauce
2 t. grated lemon peel
1/4 c. toasted sunflower seeds
3/4 c. apple juice concentrate

In small bowl, beat egg whites until fluffy. In large bowl, mix dry ingredients; stir in moist ingredients until just moistened. Fold in beaten egg whites.

Turn batter into muffin tins that have been coated with cooking spray and bake in preheated 350° oven for 25 minutes, or until wooden pick inserted in center comes out clean.

For Zucchini Bread Loaves, bake 50 minutes in two 8x4x2" loaf pans.

BAKED SCONES

1 3/4 c. whole wheat flour
1/4 c. white bean flour
2 T. dry milk powder
1 t. baking soda
1 T. baking powder
1/2 t. salt
1/2 t. cinnamon
1/2 t. ginger
2 T. canola oil or applesauce
4 t. honey
1/2 c. warm water or buttermilk

Combine dry ingredients. Stir in oil or applesauce, honey and water or milk until mixture clings to itself.

Knead dough gently on a floured surface 6 or 7 times. Divide dough into thirds. Roll each part 1/2" thick. Cut into 6 wedges.

Place on baking sheets coated with cooking spray. Bake at 450° for 10-15 minutes. Serve hot with honey butter or apple butter.

YEAST BREADS

Even though yeast breads take longer to prepare, these complete protein breads are well worth the effort. All freeze well, so take advantage of a cool day and bake up a storm.

☆☆☆ *Many bread recipes call for bean flour. See pages 4, 6, 155, 156, 172, 180 for more information on this unique method of using beans.*

See Page 6 for a Gluten-Free mix to use in these recipes in place of wheat flour.

EMMA'S BROWN AND SERVE ROLLS

3 c. warm water
2-3 t. salt
1 egg
1/4 c. canola oil or applesauce
1/4 c. molasses or honey
2 T. dry yeast
1 c. bean flour- any kind
6 -7 c. whole wheat flour

Bread Mixer: In bowl, combine 2 c. warm water with oil or applesauce, egg, salt and 3 c. flour. Mix 5 minutes at high speed in electric mixer. Let rest while combining remaining water, yeast and molasses in 4 c. mixing bowl. Allow both mixtures to rest 8-10 minutes while yeast rises double. Combine mixtures and knead at low speed, adding enough flour to make a smooth dough that starts to pull away from the sides. Knead an additional 2-3 minutes.

Turn out onto an oiled surface and pound as you knead to develop the gluten which makes a high-rising, fluffy bread. Divide dough into balls with an ice cream scoop and place in muffin tins or baking tray that have been coated with cooking spray. Cover and place on layers of toweling in a warm spot to rise double. Bake at 275° for 40 minutes. The rolls will not have browned. Remove from oven, allow to cool, remove from pans and place in freezer bags or wrap in plastic.

When ready to serve, bake on cookie sheet for 8-10 minutes at 400°.

GLUTEN FREE TAPIOCA BREAD

Adapted from recipe by Bette Hagman, "The Gluten-Free Gourmet", Henry Holt & Co, 1990.

2 c. rice flour
1 1/4 c. tapioca flour
1/4 c. white bean flour
2/3 c. dry milk powder
1 1/2 t. salt
1 1/2 T. dry yeast granules
3 1/2 t. xanthan gum
1/2 c. lukewarm water
2 t. or honey
1 t. vinegar
1/4 cup canola oil
1 1/4 c. water
3 large eggs

Combine all dry ingredients except yeast in the large bowl of a heavy duty mixer. In separate bowl, combine lukewarm water, yeast and 2 t. sugar. Add remaining moist ingredients to dry ones. Beat a few seconds. Add the dissolved yeast. Beat at highest speed for 2 minutes. Place the mixing bowl, tightly covered with plastic wrap, in a warm place and let rise until doubled. Return dough to mixer and beat 3 minutes.

Spoon dough into 2 small greased loaf pans or 1 large one, plus a few spoonfuls in greased muffin tins to bake as rolls. Let dough rise again for approximately 1 hour. Bake in preheated 400° oven for 10 minutes. Place foil over the bread and bake 50 minutes more for the large loaf, 35 minutes for small loaves, 25 minutes for rolls.

PINTO BEAN BREAD

1 pkg. dry yeast (1 T.)
1/4 c. warm water
1 c. mashed pinto beans
2 T. honey
1 T. butter or applesauce
1 egg
1 T. instant minced onion
1 t. salt
1/4 t. soda
2 1/4 to 2 1/2 c. whole wheat flour

*See Cooking Options section for "Instant Mashed Beans."

Soften yeast in water. Combine in mixing bowl with beans, honey, butter or applesauce, egg, onion, salt and soda. Add flour to form stiff dough, beating well after each addition. Cover, let rise in warm place until light and doubled in size (about 50 minutes). Stir down dough.

Turn into 1 1/2 to 2 qt. casserole that has been coated with cooking spray. Let rise till light (about 30 minutes). Bake at 350° for 40-50 minutes. Brush with soft butter and sprinkle with coarse salt.

SPELT BREAD

Spelt can be tolerated by many who are allergic to wheat. If you prefer, whole wheat flour can be used in place of spelt and xanthan gum.

2 c. spelt flour
1 c. Rita's Gluten-Free flour
2 T. dry yeast
1 t. xanthan gum
1/4 t. citric acid crystals
1/4 c. honey
2 T. oil
1 egg or 2 egg whites
1 1/2 c. warm water

Bread Machine: Place the ingredients in the baking pan of the bread maker in the order suggested in your manual. Bake on medium.

Regular Oven: Mix ingredients in the order given in the bowl of a heavy duty mixer. Mix on high speed for 3 minutes. Place bowl in a warm spot, cover with plastic wrap and a towel, and let the dough rise for approximately 1 hour, or until doubled. Return bowl to the mixer and mix on high for 3 minutes.

Knead on lightly floured board to shape loaves, adding extra flour as necessary. Place in 2 small loaf pans coated with cooking spray. Cover and let rise until doubled.

Bake in preheated 400° oven for 10 minutes. Reduce heat to 350° and bake until nicely browned, about 40-50 minutes.

HEARTY OATMEAL BREAD

1 1/2 c. boiling water
1 c. rolled oats
3/4 c. light molasses
3 T. canola oil or applesauce
2 t. salt
1 T. active dry yeast
2 c. lukewarm water
1 c. bean flour, any kind
7 c. whole wheat flour
Butter for crust

Pour boiling water over oats and let stand 30 minutes. Add molasses, oil or applesauce and salt. Dissolve yeast in warm water and add to oat mixture. Beat well. Work in enough flour to make a medium-soft dough. Turn out onto a floured board and knead until smooth, about 10 minutes. Put dough into an oiled bowl, turning to oil top of dough. Cover and let rise in a warm place until doubled, about 1 hour.

Divide and shape into 2 loaves and place in loaf pans that have been coated with cooking spray. Cover and let rise until doubled, about 45 minutes. Bake 10 minutes in preheated 400° oven. Reduce heat to 350° and bake for 30-40 minutes, or until the loaves sound hollow when tapped. Cool on wire racks. Brush the tops of the loaves with butter for a soft crust. Makes 2 loaves.

MINI OATIES

3 T. active dry yeast
1 3/4 c. warm water
1/2 c. melted honey
3 eggs
1/2 c. canola oil or applesauce
1/4 c. lentil flour
1 c. rolled oats
2 t. salt
5 to 5 1/4 c. whole wheat flour

Combine yeast, 1/2 c. water and 1 t. honey. Place remaining water, honey,oil or applesauce and 2 eggs in mixer bowl and beat. Add 3 c. flour, lentil flour, oats and salt. Beat at low speed 3 minutes. Let rest 5 min. while yeast rises double. Add yeast mixture and 2 c. flour, a little at a time. Knead 5-8 minutes. Add additional flour, as necessary, to make a soft dough that doesn't stick to your hands. Turn out on oiled counter. Pound and knead; shape into 6 balls. Place on baking sheets that have been coated with cooking spray. Cover and let rise until double, about 30-45 minutes.

Combine remaining egg and 1 T. water; brush over raised loaves. Sprinkle with sesame or poppy seeds, if desired. Bake at 375° 20-25 minutes or until loaves sound hollow when tapped lightly. Remove loaves from pan and cool on wire rack.

GOLDEN GRAINS BROWN BREAD

This recipe has been created for the Bread Machine, but can be made in a regular oven.

1 T. yeast
1 1/2 c. brown rice flour
3/4 c. potato starch flour
1/2 c. tapioca flour
2 1/2 t. xanthan gum
1/2 c. pinto bean flour
2 T. Teff flour
1/3 c. fine cornmeal or corn flour
1/4 t. citric acid
1 1/2 t. salt
1/4 c. honey
1/4 c. canola oil or applesauce
1 egg + 1 egg white
1 2/3 c. water

Place the ingredients in the baking pan of the bread maker in the order suggested in your manual. Bake on medium.

To bake in a regular oven, mix ingredients in the order given in the bowl of a heavy duty mixer. Mix on high speed for 3 minutes. Place bowl in a warm spot, cover with plastic wrap and a towel, and let the dough rise for approximately 1 hour, or until doubled. Return bowl to the mixer and mix on high for 3 minutes.

Mixture will be like cookie dough. Spoon into 2-3 small loaf pans coated with cooking spray. Cover and let rise until doubled. Bake in preheated 400° oven for 10 minutes. Reduce heat to 350° and bake until nicely browned, about 40-50 minutes.

CHEESE 'N ONION BREAD

1 T. active dry yeast
1/3 c. warm water
1 T. honey
1 c. warm water
2 T. canola oil or applesauce
3 c. whole wheat flour
1/2 c. lentil flour
1 env. Lipton Onion Soup Mix
1 t. salt (opt.)
1 1/4 c. shredded Cheddar cheese

Melted butter

Mix yeast, 1/3 c. water and honey. Let rise to double. Meanwhile, in mixing bowl, add lentil flour and 2 c. wheat flour to water and oil or applesauce and mix 5 minutes. Add yeast mixture and remaining ingredients except cheese and butter, adding only enough flour until dough pulls away from sides of bowl. Knead 5 minutes. Turn onto oiled counter and knead and beat 1 minute.

Roll into 10" x 8" rectangle; sprinkle with 1 c. cheese. Roll, starting at smaller side; pinch ends to seal. Brush with melted butter and sprinkle with remaining cheese. Cut roll into 1" slices and bake with sides touching on a baking sheet that has been coated with cooking spray for 18-20 minutes, or until browned.

CRUSTY MINI-WHEATS

1/4 c. warm water
2 T. active dry yeast
2 T. honey
1 1/4 c. warm water
1 1/2 t. salt
1/4 c. canola oil or applesauce
3 T. dry milk powder
1/2 c. pinto bean flour
2 1/2 to 3 c. whole wheat flour
Sesame oil and sesame seeds

Combine 1/4 c. warm water, yeast and honey. In mixing bowl, combine remaining ingredients and 1/2 of the flour. Mix well, let rest while yeast rises to double. Add yeast mixture, then remaining flour a little at a time, adding only enough to make a smooth dough.

Cut and shape into 4 mini-loaves; place on baking sheet that has been coated with cooking spray. Cover and allow to rise double in a warm place.

Option: If desired, brush loaves with a mixture of 2 t. fat-free mayonnaise, 1 t. vegetable oil, 1/4 t. flavored sesame oil and sprinkle with sesame seeds. Bake at 375° 30-40 minutes, or until golden brown.

SPOTTED TURTLE BREAD

1 1/8 c. warm water
1 T. honey
1 T. yeast
3 1/2-4 1/2 c. sifted whole wheat flour
3/4 c. cooked, mashed black beans
1 c. ea. dried raisins and chopped nuts
1 1/2 T. canola oil or applesauce
1/2 t. salt

In a large mixing bowl, mix 1/2 c. of the warm water with honey and yeast and let rest about 10 minutes, until yeast has doubled. Meanwhile, mix 2 cups flour with remaining water and mix in bread mixer, with hand mixer or by hand for 2-5 minutes. Let rest 10 minutes, then add yeast mixture and remaining ingredients alternately, adding only as much flour as necessary to make a soft, not sticky, dough.

Turn dough out onto floured board and knead 1-2 minutes, then shape into small "turtle" rolls and place, sides touching, in oiled or buttered 9"x13" baking dish. Cover and let rise until very light, more than doubled in bulk, about 1 hour or more. Bake at 400° about 20 minutes for small turtles, up to 45 minutes for large turtles, or until golden brown.

DRESSINGS

Most of these dressings are NOT made with beans, although regular mayonnaise in a recipe could be replaced with tofu or soy mayonnaise.

All recipes are Gluten-Free, when made with GF vinegar and seasonings.

This section is included for those who want a better-for-you alternative to the chemicals and preservatives in commercial dressings.

These dressings are all excellent served with the recipes in the salad section.

FAVORITE BUTTERMILK RANCH DRESSING

*2 c. mayonnaise**
2 c. buttermilk
1/2 t. garlic powder
2 t. dried onion flakes
2 T. parsley flakes
1 t. black pepper
1 t. salt or substitute
1 1/2 t. onion powder

*Soy mayonnaise, cholesterol-free, homemade or commercial mayonnaise can be used. If fat-free mayonnaise is used, reduce amount to 1 c. and increase buttermilk to 3 c.

Combine ingredients in order given, whisking until smooth. Makes 1 qt.

For **SPICY BUTTERMILK RANCH**, add 3 T. Picante sauce.

BLENDER MAYONNAISE

2 eggs or 4 egg whites
1 tsp. salt
1 1/2 - 1 3/4 cups vegetable oil
2 T. lemon juice
2 T. white vinegar
1/8 t. of white pepper

Blend all except 3/4 c. oil until smooth. On high speed, slowly add the oil in a steady pencil-thin stream. Refrigerate and use within 1 week. **Low-cal** - Make 1/2 batch and stir in 1 c. plain low-fat yogurt. Makes about 2 cups.

SOY MAYONNAISE

Blend:
1 c. tofu
1/2 c. soy milk
3/4 t. salt
2 T. lemon juice
1 T. vinegar
1/4 t. onion powder
3/4 c. vegetable oil

Blend all but oil, then continue blending and add oil slowly until mixture thickens. Makes about 2 cups.

CREAMY DRESSING

1 cup yogurt sour cream (or 1 c. yogurt)
1/4 c. fat-free mayonnaise
1 t. honey
1 T. vinegar
1/4 t. Worcestershire sauce

Mix well. Makes 1 1/4 cups.

EASY THOUSAND ISLAND DRESSING

2 c. fat-free mayonnaise
1 c. catsup
2 T. minced pickles or relish
1/2 c. tofu
1/4 c. milk or buttermilk

Whisk ingredients together to form a smooth paste. Makes about 3 cups.

CUCUMBER DRESSING

1 medium cucumber
1 t. grated onion
2 t. chopped fresh parsley
1 t. lemon juice
3/4 c. buttermilk
1 c. fat-free mayonnaise
1/2 t. salt
coarse black pepper to taste

Finely grate peeled and seeded cucumber; drain and combine with other ingredients. Chill. Makes 2 cups.

ORIENTAL DRESSING

1/2 c. canola oil or chicken broth
2 T. brown sugar
1 1/2 t. prepared mustard
1 t. catsup
2 T. soy sauce
2 t. vinegar
1 1/2 t. ginger
1 T. sesame seeds

Mix all ingredients and store unused portion in refrigerator. Great on green or pasta salads. Makes about 1 cup.

SALADS

Salads made with the addition of beans make a filling meal or side dish. Most of these salad recipes are classed as complete proteins, as they contain a grain or a dairy product.

Keep cooked beans on hand in the refrigerator, freezer, or pressure bottled in jars on the pantry shelf.

When a recipe calls for cooked, mashed beans, see the Cooking Options Section for instructions to make "instant mashed beans" in only 5 minutes from bean flour and boiling water.

Most salad recipes are Gluten-Free. Check the Recipe Index if unsure.

MEXI-PITA BAR

3 whole wheat pita bread loaves, halved
Filling:
2 c. cooked garbanzo beans
1/4 t. cumin
1/4 t. salt
1/4 t. garlic powder
1/2 c. finely chopped onion

Heat through.

Toppings:
1/2 c. salsa or taco sauce
1 c. chopped tomato
1/2 c. plain yogurt or sour cream)
2 c. shredded lettuce
1 c. grated jack cheese

Arrange salad-bar style and allow each person to spoon 1/2 c. heated filling mixture into each pocket halves and his/her choice of toppings.

Makes 6 sandwiches.

PICNIC SALAD

2 c. cold, cooked kidney beans
4 c. cold, cooked brown rice
1 c. chopped celery
1 sm. green pepper, chopped
1 c. chopped cucumber
1 tomato, diced
2 green onions, chopped
1/2 c. fat-free mayonnaise
1 t. prepared mustard
salt to taste

Combine all ingredients. Serve on lettuce lined platter, if desired. OR, place 1/2 c. salad in a large lettuce leaf, roll, and serve as a Walking Picnic Salad!

Serves 4-6.

RED AND WHITE PASTA SALAD

1 1/2 c. cooked red beans
1 1/2 c. cooked lima or navy beans
1 1/2 c. cooked pasta
1 t. finely minced green onion
1/2 c. thinly sliced celery
ranch or italian dressing

Combine cooled beans and mix lightly with all other ingredients. Place salad greens on a plate and heap bean mixture in center. Serves 4-6.

WHOLE MEAL LAYERED SALAD

1 small head lettuce, shredded
1 c. cooked red or pink beans
1 c. sliced fresh mushrooms
1 c. chopped green pepper
1 c. cooked garbanzo beans
1/2 c. chopped green onions
1 c. grated sweet potato or carrots
2 c. frozen peas, thawed
1 hard cooked egg, diced
1 1/4 c. fat-free mayonnaise + 2 T. milk
1 c. alfalfa sprouts or buckwheat lettuce

In a large glass bowl, layer in order given. Mix milk with mayonnaise and spread over egg, "sealing" salad. Top with sprouts or buckwheat lettuce. If desired, top with 1 1/2 c. grated cheddar cheese. Cover and refrigerate for 1 hour or overnight.

GARBANZO BEAN AND TOFU SALAD

1 c. cooked garbanzo beans
1/2 c. tofu
1/3 c. fat-free mayonnaise
2 t. diced onion
1 t. diced green pepper
1/2 c. thinly sliced celery
1 T. soy sauce
1/8 t. garlic powder
1 T. chicken or vegetable soup base
pepper to taste

Mash beans and tofu with a fork. Add remaining ingredients and mix well. Use as a sandwich filling or serve on lettuce leaves and/or sprouts.

WHEAT CURRY SALAD

1/2 c. tomato juice
1 t. curry powder
2 t. chicken or vegetable soup base
1 1/2 c. cooked cracked wheat
1/2 c. cooked pinto beans

Heat juice and seasonings to boiling; add cracked wheat and beans. Cover and simmer 3 minutes. Add:

1/4 c. finely chopped onions
1/2 c. finely chopped green pepper
3/4 c. fat-free mayonnaise

Mix well and chill. Serves 5.

CHILI RICE SALAD

2 c. cooked brown rice
1 c. cooked red beans
1/2 c. grated cheese
1/2 t. cumin
1 t. chicken or vegetable soup base
1/2 c. diced celery
2 T. chopped onions
1/2 c. fat-free mayonnaise

Combine all ingredients; serve on a bed of lettuce and sprouts, topped with additional grated cheese and diced tomatoes, if desired.

DIETER'S DELIGHT

2 carrots, grated fine
3 stalks celery, sliced thin
1/4 c. cooked brown rice or cracked wheat
1/4 c. cooked red beans
2 tomatoes, diced
2 T. sesame seeds
dash ginger
2 t. shoyu or soy sauce

Combine and serve. If you need a dressing, add 2 T. Buttermilk Dressing. Serves 2.

LENTIL SALAD

3 c. barely cooked lentils, cooled
4 T. olive oil or 1/3 c. vegetable broth
1 small onion, chopped
1 clove garlic, mashed
3 tomatoes, chopped
1 t. oregano
salt to taste
1/8 t. cayenne pepper
1 T. chopped fresh basil
1-2 T. chopped fresh parsley
3 T. lemon juice

In a skillet, heat 2 T. of the oil or broth and saute onion, garlic and tomatoes for 1 minute. Add to remaining ingredients and mix gently. Add salt to taste and cool. Serves 6-8.

TANGY PASTA AND BEANS

3 c. cooked pink or red beans
2 c. cooked macaroni, drained
1 c. thinly sliced celery
One 4 1/2 oz. cans chopped olives
salt and white pepper to taste
1 c. chopped fresh tomatoes
1/2 c. chopped green pepper
1 t. chopped fresh parsley
2 T. olive oil (opt.)
1/4 c. lemon juice

Mix oil, if used, lemon juice, salt and pepper and add to remaining ingredients. Serve at room temperature or chilled.

MEXICAN DINNER IN A PITA

1 medium head iceberg lettuce or Napa Cabbage, coarsely shredded
1 small onion, diced
1 red bell pepper, diced
2 c. cooked pinto or kidney beans
3 T. Pace's Picante Sauce
2 tomatoes, diced
1/2 t. ground cumin
Ranch Dressing
1/2 c. toasted sunflower seeds
2 Pita Pockets, halved

Mix all but dressing and sun seeds. Put 1/4 of mixture in each Pita half. Top with Ranch dressing and toasted seeds. Serves 4.

CREAMY TUNA SALAD

1 c. mashed pinto or white beans
1 c. chopped celery
1 can (6 1/2 oz) water packed tuna
1 green onion, chopped
2 T. plain yogurt
2 T. fat-free mayonnaise
1-3 T. Pace's Picante sauce OR 1 t. chicken or vegetable soup base

Drain tuna, mix into remaining ingredients and serve on lettuce leaves, or make sandwiches or spread on toasted wheat bread. For Hot Tuna Sandwiches, spread mixture on wheat bread and broil until bubbly. Serve hot.

BEAN SPROUT 'N RICE SALAD

3 c. cold cooked brown rice
1/2 c. chopped green onion tops
2 t. chopped fresh parsley
1/2 c. mung bean sprouts
3 T. lemon juice
2 T. olive oil

Chop bean sprouts and add to remaining ingredients. Chill and serve. Add salt to taste. Serves 4-6. Can be served on a bed of fresh lettuce or alfalfa sprouts.

MARINATED BEAN SALAD

2 c. cooked garbanzo beans
2 c. cooked red or kidney beans
2 c. cooked green beans
2 T. finely chopped onion

***

Whisk together:
1 T. ea. vinegar and lemon juice
3/4 t. paprika
1/2 t. salt
1/8 c. cold water or bean liquid
1/4 c. honey
1 T. vegetable oil (opt.)

Pour dressing over beans and add 1 T. sesame seeds, if desired. Chill overnight, or if you're in a hurry, serve immediately.

ONE AND ONE-HALF BEAN SALAD

1/2 c. sprouted cooked white beans
1/2 c. sprouted cooked kidney beans
1 c. grated carrot
1 c. grated cucumber
6 T. fat-free mayonnaise
1/4 t. celery salt
2 T. mild Picante sauce
salt and pepper to taste, if desired

Finely mince white beans so one bean is half hidden! Combine remaining ingredients and stir well to mix dressing. Serves 4.

LIZZY'S ORIENTAL SALAD

1 pkg. Ramen Noodles with chicken flavoring
3/4 c. water
1/4 c. onion, chopped
2 T. sesame seeds
4 c. shredded napa cabbage
1/4 c. chopped cooked garbanzo beans
2 T. honey
2 T. canola oil (opt.)
salt and pepper to taste
1/2 c. finely chopped almonds

Bring water to a boil and cook noodles for 6 minutes; add seasoning. Drain off any excess water. Cool and add remaining ingredients, with almonds reserved to top each individual serving. Serves 4.

MEDITERRANEAN SALAD

3 c. cooked lima beans, cooled
2 c. coarsely grated zucchini
2 T. sliced green onion
1/4 c. chopped ripe olives
1 T. chopped pimiento
1/2 c. grated Jack cheese
Leaf lettuce
Caesar salad dressing
Optional - 1 c. cooked pasta

Combine all ingredients except lettuce and dressing; toss lightly. Serve on lettuce-lined plates. Serves 4-6.

FRESH GARDEN SALAD

2 c. cooked, cooled baby lima or kidney beans, or a combination
1/4 c. chopped ripe olives
2 tomatoes, sliced in wedges
1 c. cooked green beans
1 medium carrot, shredded
1 large cucumber, sliced
Ranch dressing to taste

Combine all ingredients and mix lightly. Serve on lettuce leaves or sprouts. Serves 4.

CRUNCHY BABY LIMA AND CHEDDAR SLAW

3 cups shredded cabbage
1 T. minced green onion
1 2/3 c. cooked lima beans
1/8 t. garlic salt
4 oz. cheddar cheese, cubed
1/4 c. Creamy Dressing
1 t. lemon juice
Romaine leaves

Add combined ingredients to lettuce-lined bowl.

Creamy Dressing: Combine ***1 cup sour cream*** (or 1 c. yogurt and omit vinegar), ***1/4 c. fat-free mayonnaise, 2 T. vinegar, 1 t. honey*** and ***1/4 t. Worcestershire sauce.*** Mix well.

(Adapted from a recipe published by the Baby Lima Council of the California Dry Bean Advisory Board.)

OVERNIGHT BEAN SALAD

1 c. cooked kidney beans
1 c. cooked white or navy beans
1 t. chopped celery
1/4 c. chopped green onions
1 c. chopped fresh parsley (for garnish)

Dressing:
3 T. olive oil
1/4 t. prepared mustard
1 T. lemon juice
1/2 t. light honey

Mix all ingredients except parsley and chill 1 hour or overnight. Serve with fresh parsley garnish.

RED PEPPER SALAD

1 small red bell pepper, diced
1 c. cooked lentils or brown rice
2 c. chopped celery
1 c. sliced fresh mushrooms (optional)
1/2 c. diced onion
1 t. chicken or vegetable base to taste
French or Ranch Dressing to taste

Mix all ingredients and serve on lettuce leaves or sprouts. Serves 4.

GARBANZO BEAN SALAD

1/2 c. chopped onion
2 c. cooked garbanzo beans
2 tomatoes, chopped
1 medium cucumber, chopped
1 small zucchini, cut into matchstick-size strips
1/2 small clove garlic, minced
3 T. lemon juice
4 T. olive oil (opt.)
salt and pepper to taste

Arrange zucchini strips on 4 serving plates. Mix remaining ingredients and place on zucchini strips (or use strips as garnish for top of salad). Serves 4.

CHINESE GARBANZO BEAN SALAD

1 c. chopped mung bean sprouts
1/2 c. chopped green pepper
2 t. fresh parsley, chopped
1 t. chopped green onions
2 c. cooked garbanzo beans
1 tomato, diced
1/4 c. dressing

Mix all ingredients and serve chilled.

Dressing:

1/2 c. canola oil (opt.)
2 T. brown sugar
1 1/2 t. prepared mustard
1 t. catsup
2 T. soy sauce
2 t. vinegar
1 1/2 t. ginger
1 T. sesame seeds

Mix all ingredients and store unused portion in refrigerator.

BEANS 'N RICE SALAD

1 red pepper, sliced in strips
1 green pepper, diced
2 c. cooked brown rice
1/2 c. cooked pink or white beans
1 small cucumber, diced
2 green onions, diced
One 4 1/2 oz. can chopped olives
Italian or Ranch Dressing to taste

Reserve red pepper for garnish. Mix remaining ingredients and serve plain or atop fresh lettuce leaves or sprouts.

Serves 4.

SPANISH RICE SALAD

4 med-small tomatoes
2 green onions, chopped
2 t. fresh parsley, chopped
2 c. cooked brown rice
1/2 c. chopped red pepper
1 c. cooked kidney beans
2 T c. olive oil (opt.)
1/2 t. chili powder
2 T. Pace's Picante Sauce
1-2 t. vegetable soup base
1 c. grated mozzarella cheese (opt)

Cut tops off tomatoes and scoop out centers. Add to remaining ingredients and fill tomatoes.

Garnish with grated mozzarella cheese, if desired.

ORIENTAL CASHEW PASTA SALAD

2 c. cooked noodles, any kind
1 tomato, diced
2 T. sesame seeds, toasted
1 T. chopped green onions
1 c. cashews, chopped and toasted
1 c. 2-day bean sprouts (or 3 c. 3" purchased bean sprouts)
*1/4 t. sesame oil**
1 T. soy sauce
2 T. lemon juice

*Flavored oil found in oriental section of supermarket

Mix oil, soy sauce and lemon juice and pour over remaining ingredients. Toss lightly.

AVOCADO BEAN SALAD

2 c. cooked brown rice
2 ripe avocados, diced
1 c. cooked lima or pinto beans
2 hard boiled eggs, diced (opt.)
3 medium tomatoes, diced
1 c. fresh mushrooms, sliced
3 green onions, chopped
French or Ranch dressing to taste

Gently mix all ingredients. If desired, serve on fresh spinach or lettuce leaves.

Serves 4-6.

SUNCHOKE SALAD

1 lb. Sunchokes (Jerusalem Artichokes) peeled and grated
1 c. cooked kidney beans
1 c. chopped celery
1 c. frozen peas, thawed
1 t. lemon juice
Ranch dressing to taste

Mix lemon juice with grated Sunchokes and mix with remaining ingredients. (Note: Sunchokes are sold in most grocery stores and can be planted like potatoes, but be careful, because they multiply like rabbits!!)

Serves 4-6.

SPEEDY GONZALES BEAN AND CUCUMBER SALAD

2 cucumbers, diced
1 c. cooked kidney beans
1 c. diced celery
2 T. mild Pace's Picante Sauce
4 T. fat-free mayonnaise

Combine all ingredients.

Serves 2-4.

CUCUMBER SALAD

2 lg. tomatoes, diced
3 6" cucumbers, diced
1/2 c. sliced fresh mushrooms
1 4 oz. can chopped olives
2 T. mild Picante sauce
1 1/2 c. cooked brown rice
1/2 c. cooked red beans
Buttermilk Dressing

Combine all ingredients, adding dressing to taste. Serve on lettuce or sprout lined plates.

This is also excellent with zucchini instead of cucumbers.

PETITE PEAS AND BEAN SALAD

16 oz. pkg. frozen petite peas, partially thawed
1 T. chopped green onions
3 chopped eggs
1/8 t. prepared mustard
3-4 T. fat-free mayonnaise
2 T. chopped olives
1 T. chicken or vegetable soup base
1/2 c. cooked red beans
1/2 c. cooked brown rice

Put all into a bowl and mix well. Serve cold.

GREEN BEAN AND OLIVE SALAD

1 c. diced celery
4 c. cooked green beans, drained
1 4 oz. can chopped olives
2 tomatoes, diced
1/2 c. cooked red beans
Spicy Buttermilk Dressing *(see p. 31)*

Mix lightly and spoon onto lettuce-lined serving plates. Top with dressing to taste.

FRESH ZUCCHINI SALAD

1 c. diced celery
1 c. diced tomato
1/2 c. cooked red beans
2 c. diced or shredded zucchini
2 T. fresh minced onion
1 c. Buttermilk Dressing (see p. 31)
1 4 1/2 oz. can chopped olives
1 T. mild Picante Sauce

Mix well and serve on a bed of lettuce or alfalfa sprouts.

CREAMY HOT BEAN SALAD

2 c. cooked lima beans
1 T. chopped green onions
1/2 c. sliced mushrooms
1/3 c. yogurt sour cream
1-2 t. vegetable soup base

In a small saucepan, cook mushrooms in 2 T. boiling water for 5 min. Add remaining ingredients, adding base to taste. Serve hot or cold, atop crisp lettuce leaves.

Serves 4.

MUNG SPROUT SALAD

4 c. 3" long mung sprouts
2 green onions, chopped
1 rib celery, diced
1 small red pepper, chopped
1 small cucumber, diced
1 T. sesame seeds

Dressing:
2 t. soy sauce
1/2 t. light honey
1/2 t. salt
1 T. vinegar
1/2 t. prepared mustard
1/8 t. ground ginger
2 T. olive oil (opt.)

Combine salad ingredients, mix dressing and serve. Serves 4-6.

SPEEDY MEXI-BEAN SALAD

2 c. cooked pinto beans
1 c. cooked brown rice
1 c. diced celery
1 small diced green pepper
1/4 t. ground cumin
3 T. Pace's Picante Sauce
2-3 T. fat-free mayonnaise
1-2 t.chicken soup base, to taste

Combine all ingredients and serve on lettuce, sprouts, or in a pita pocket.

Serves 4.

VEGETABLE BEAN SALAD

2 c. cooked elbow macaroni
1 c. cooked white beans
1/2 c. plain yogurt
2 T. onion, finely chopped
2 ribs celery, chopped
1/3 c. grated raw carrots
1/4 c. fat-free mayonnaise
2 t. cider vinegar or lemon juice
1/2 t. prepared mustard
1 t. chicken or vegetable soup base

Combine all ingredients and serve plain or on salad greens.

Serves 4-6.

RED BEAN SALAD

3 to 4 c. torn salad greens
1 can (6 1/2 oz.) water packed tuna
1 c. diced celery
1 green onion, chopped
2 c. cooked red beans
1 carrot, grated or sliced thinly

Combine celery, onion, beans and carrot and toss lightly. Place on salad greens and top with chunks of tuna.

Serves 4. Top with Buttermilk Dressing if desired.

COMPANY SALAD BAR

Set out a variety of the following and let guests build their own!

Beans - cooked kidney, garbanzo, pinto, pink, black turtle, blackeye, anasazi, (or whatever kind is available) and cooked green beans

Grains - cooked brown rice, white rice, cracked wheat (omit for GF recipe)

Misc. Protein - grated cheese, cottage cheese, tofu (fresh chunks or sauteéd), drained tuna, black olives, toasted sesame and sunflower seeds, Bacon Bits, boiled eggs

Greens - alfalfa sprouts, buckwheat lettuce, mung sprouts, fresh parsley or watercress, spinach leaves, napa cabbage

Other veggies - chopped celery, diced or shredded carrots, green and white onions, Jerusalem artichokes, Jicama, tomatoes, zucchini, cucumber, water chestnuts, slivered raw yams (matchstick size), sliced mushrooms, red and green bell peppers, radishes, cauliflower, broccoli (use the peeled stems, too), grated or diced zucchini, tomatoes, pickles

Dressings - Buttermilk Ranch (see p. 31), Picante Sauce, Italian, Sweet and Sour sauce, (see p. 59), French, etc. etc.

SPICY BLACK BEAN TACO SALAD

1 large tomato, chopped
1 small red/green bell pepper
3 green onions, chopped fine
1 4 1/2 oz. can chopped olives
1/2 c. cooked brown rice
3 c. cooked, drained black beans
1/2 c. alfalfa sprouts
1 head shredded romaine lettuce
1 c. grated cheese (opt.)
corn chips or flour tortillas

Mix salad ingredients and place over corn chips. Or wrap in heated flour tortillas or spoon into pita pockets. Top with Taco Sauce or Spicy Hot Ranch Dressing.

SWEET AND SOUR LENTIL SALAD

1 c. cooked lentils
1/2 medium onion, minced
2 c. chopped cucumber
1/2 c. chopped green pepper
1 T. sesame seeds
1 c. thinly sliced celery
1/4 c. cider vinegar
1/8 t. white pepper (opt)
2 t. light honey
1 T. soy sauce

Combine all ingredients. If time permits, chill 3-4 hours. If not, serve anyway!

Serves 4-6.

EASY LAYERED SPINACH SALAD

4 c. torn spinach leaves
2 c. cooked red beans
1 c. cooked lima beans
2 boiled eggs, mashed with a fork
Toasted sunflower seeds
Buttermilk dressing (see p. 31)

Atop crisp spinach leaves on individual plates, layer beans, eggs and seeds. Serve topped with Buttermilk Dressing.

Serves 4.

LIMA BEAN SALAD

2 c. cooked lima beans
1/4 c. minced onion
1/2 c. minced dill pickles
1/4 c. fat-free mayonnaise
1/4 c. Picante Sauce
1/2 to 1 t. chicken or vegetable soup base

Combine all ingredients. Serve on crisp lettuce, sprouts or in a hollowed out tomato or cucumber.

Serves 4.

SOYBEAN TUNA SALAD

2 c. cooked cracked soybeans
1 large tomato, diced
1/4 c. cooked brown rice or cracked wheat
1 6 1/2 oz. can tuna, drained
1/2 c. finely chopped celery
1/4 c. green pepper, chopped
1/3 c. Buttermilk dressing

Toss lightly and serve on salad greens or sprouts.

Serves 4.

TOFU CURRY SALAD

1 lb. tofu
3 t. soy sauce
1/4 t. garlic powder
1/2 t. chicken or vegetable soup base
1/3 c. chopped celery
1/2 c. cooked brown rice
1/3 c. fat-free mayonnaise
1 t. curry powder
1/2 t. dry mustard powder
dash cayenne
1/4 c. chopped green onion
1 T. toasted sesame seeds

Mash tofu and stir all ingredients together with a fork, blending well. Serve in a mound on a bed of salad greens or sprouts, or as a sandwich filling or chip dip.

Serves 4-6.

RICE AND BEAN SALAD

1/2 c. fat-free mayonnaise
1/4 c. catsup
1/2 c. diced green pepper
1 1/2 c. diced celery
1/2 c. diced green onions
6 1/2 oz. can drained tuna
1 1/2 c. cooked brown rice
1/2 c. cooked garbanzo beans

Mix all ingredients together. Serve on a bed of lettuce or sprouts. OR, fill pita pockets.

Serves 4-6.

DIPS AND SANDWICH FILLINGS

These high-protein dips and sandwich fillings are perfect for snacks or even an entire meal. They are full of nutritious ingredients, contain very little fat, little or no cholesterol, AND, they are easy and fast to make.

Most recipes are Gluten-Free when served with Gluten-Free Bread.

When a recipe calls for cooked, mashed beans, refer to the Cooking Options Section for "Instant Mashed Beans."

MEXICAN HOT POCKETS

1/4 c. water
1/2 c. chopped onion
1/2 c. cooked brown rice or cracked wheat
1 c. salsa or taco sauce
1 1/2 c. cooked red beans
1/2 t. ea. basil, oregano, chili powder, cumin
2 t. chicken or vegetable soup base
2 c. shredded lettuce
1 c. chopped tomato
2 c. shredded cheddar cheese
3 whole wheat pitas, halved

*See Cooking Options to cook dry, fluffy cracked wheat

Simmer onions in water and sauce 2 minutes. Add beans, wheat, 1 c. of the cheese and seasonings. Heat through. Spoon 1/2 c. mixture into each pita pocket half. Top with lettuce, tomato, remaining cheese and additional salsa, if desired. This is also good topped with a spoonful of yogurt or sour cream. (See Bette Hagman's "More From The Gluten-Free Gourmet" for GF Pita Bread.)

TUNA-BEAN SANDWICH FILLING

1/2 c. flaked tuna
1 c. cooked, mashed white beans
1 T. grated onion
1/2 t. lemon juice
1/4 c. chopped celery
2 T. green chiles, chopped
1 t. chicken or vegetable soup base
Dash of pepper
1/4 c. fat-free mayonnaise

Combine ingredients. Serve chilled on toasted bread, in a pita pocket, or spread on bread or whole pita and broil until bubbly. Top with cheese, if desired. Makes 4-6 sandwiches. (See Bette Hagman's "More From The Gluten-Free Gourmet" for GF Pita Bread.)

CHEESEY BEAN DIP

1 c. cottage cheese, drained
1-2 T. Picante Sauce
1/4 c. chopped olives
2 t. chicken or vegetable soup base
3/4 c. cooked, mashed beans
1/4 c. chopped onion
1/2 c. cooked brown rice or cracked wheat

Blend cottage cheese, base and beans until smooth. Add other ingredients and blend just until mixed. Makes about 3 cups.
Note: Use white, pinto or pink beans.

GUACAMOLE

1 large, ripe avocado, mashed
1 medium tomato, diced (opt.)
1/4 c. cooked split peas(see below)*
1/4 c. fat-free mayonnaise
1 t. onion, finely chopped
2 t. lemon juice
1/4 t. chili powder

Mix all and serve with sliced veggies or your choice of crackers. If desired, add 1/4 c. Picante Sauce.

**Fast Method* - Stir together 1/4 c. finely ground pea flour and 1 c. warm water. (See Cooking Options.) Bring to a boil, while stirring. When thick, (about 30 seconds), turn heat to low and cook 3 minutes. Freeze in 1/4 c. portions to add to soups or to use for Guacamole Dip.

BEANAMOLE

1 large, ripe avocado, mashed
1 lg. tomato, diced
1 c. cooked garbanzo beans
1/4 c. fat-free mayonnaise
1 t. onion, finely chopped
1 t. lemon juice
2 T. mild Picante sauce
salt or vegetable seasoning to taste

Mash beans slightly and add remaining ingredients. Mix well. Serve with sliced veggies or crackers.

ONION DIP

1 lb. tofu
1 env. Lipton instant onion soup mix
2 t. lemon juice
1 T. chopped green onions
2 T. chopped ripe olives

Blend tofu, soup mix and lemon juice until smooth. Add green onions and olives. Chill and serve.

BROILED BEAN AND TUNA SANDWICHES

1 6 1/2 oz. can drained tuna
1/2 c. cooked red beans, mashed
1 c. low or no-fat cottage cheese
2 T. fat-free mayonnaise
3 T. Picante Sauce

Mix all ingredients and spread on rolls, gluten-free or whole wheat bread, or whole wheat flour tortillas. Broil until mixture is bubbly. Serve hot.

CHEESEY SANDWICHES

1/4 c. dried parmesan cheese
1/2 c. cooked brown rice or cracked wheat
1/2 c. crumbled tofu
1 c. yellow grated cheese
1/2 c. sprouted mung beans
1/3 c. chopped dill pickles

Mix all ingredients together. Spoon onto toasted gluten-free or whole wheat bread. Broil until bubbly. Serve hot or cold, OR, omit sprouts and serve as a chip dip.

FRESH SPINACH SANDWICH

1 lb. fresh spinach
1/4 lb. fresh mushrooms
2 hard cooked eggs
1 c. cooked garbanzo beans
1 t. lemon juice
1/4 c. chopped green onions
soy bacon bits
toasted sunflower seeds

Wash and drain spinach; tear into bite-size pieces. Clean and slice mushrooms. Finely chop eggs. Add beans, lemon juice and dressing and toss lightly. Fill pita pockets (or spoon onto toasted rye, gluten-free or wheat bread) and sprinkle with green onions, bacon bits and sunflower seeds.

GARBANZO BEAN SANDWICH SPREAD

1 c. cooked garbanzo beans
2 T. fat-free mayonnaise
1 T. pickle relish
2 T. minced green onion
salt or vegetable soup base to taste

Mash beans and whip with mayonnaise. Add remaining ingredients.

Serve on toasted bread.

CREAMY AVOCADO SANDWICH

1 lg. avocado
1/2 c. cooked garbanzo beans
2-3 T. fat-free mayonnaise
4 slices toasted bread
salt or vegetable seasoning broth powder to taste

Mash peeled avocado and beans. Add seasoning and mayonnaise.

Spread on toasted bread and serve as an open-face sandwich, or add lettuce and sprouts and top with another piece of toasted bread. Or, serve in a pita pocket.

TOASTY BEANERS

4 slices toasted bread, flour tortillas or whole pitas
3 c. cooked red or pinto beans
1-2 T. mild Picante Sauce
2 T. fat-free mayonnaise
1 c. grated cheese or cottage cheese

Mix all ingredients and place on bread. Broil or microwave until bubbly.

SPICY CUCUMBER DIP

1 medium cucumber
*1 c. mashed white beans**
1/2 c. cream cheese
1/2 t. chili powder
1/4 c. fat-free mayonnaise
2 t. mild Picante Sauce
Vegetable seasoning broth to taste

* See Cooking Options to make "instant mashed beans".

Peel cucumber and blend until smooth with all other ingredients.

Serve with carrot sticks, yam slices or chips.

EASY BEAN DIP

2 c. cooked pinto beans
2 T. mild Picante Sauce
salt or seasoning to taste

Mash beans, add Picante Sauce and whip until smooth. (Or, see Cooking Options for "Instant Mashed Beans" recipe.) Add grated cheese, if desired.

Great as a sandwich spread, topped with cheese and broiled until bubbly.

RED AND WHITE BROILED SANDWICHES

3 c. cooked red beans
1 t. chicken or vegetable soup base
3 T. mild Picante Sauce
1 1/2 c. grated white cheese

Mix all but cheese. Spread on toasted bread or pita pockets. Sprinkle generously with cheese.

Broil until bubbly.

BEANY TUNA DELIGHT

6 1/2 oz. can drained tuna
1/2 c. chopped celery
1 c. cooked lima beans
1 c. cooked brown rice
1 sm. onion, chopped
1/3 c. fat-free mayonnaise
1 lg. chopped tomato
1 c. cottage cheese

Slightly mash lima beans and mix all ingredients well.

Serve cold as a salad or filling, or broiled on toasted bread or on (or in) pita pockets.

TOMATO BEAN FILLING OR SALAD

2 ripe tomatoes, diced
2 T. chopped ripe olives
1 c. cooked kidney beans
1/4 c. cooked brown rice
1/2 c. sliced water chestnuts
2 T. mild Pace's Picante Sauce
2 T. fat-free mayonnaise (opt.)

Mix and fill pita pockets. OR, serve on a bed of lettuce and top with fresh alfalfa sprouts.

Serves 4.

WHITE BEAN SPREAD

2 T. diced cooked pimientos
2 T. fat-free mayonnaise (opt.)
2 c. cooked white beans, mashed
garlic powder and salt to taste

Mix and spread on toasted whole grain bread. Or, fill pita pockets with bean mixture and leaf lettuce.

Serves 4.

SAUCES AND GRAVIES

Just imagine a creamy white gravy, or a rich tamale pie gravy – with NO FAT! We've all heard how fattening sauces and gravies are and that we should eliminate them to cut down on our calories. Many are allergic to milk and thought that meant they must eliminate white sauce or gravy.

Not so! Finely ground white bean flour creates a thick gravy that appears to have been made with many fattening ingredients! With a base of vegetable or chicken broth, you can add bean flour and seasonings to make 3-minute gravies that are GOOD for you. ***Use them often!***

All recipes in this section are Gluten-Free.

ORIENTAL SAUCE

Serve over rice, stir-fried veggies, or pasta.

1 c. soy sauce
1 t. chicken or vegetable soup base
1/4 t. pepper
2 t. white bean flour
3/4 c. water
2 T. honey
1/2 t. molasses

In a small saucepan, whisk together sauce ingredients, and cook 2 minutes over medium heat. For thicker sauce, add 3-4 T. cornstarch and cook until thick.

SWEET AND SOUR SAUCE

1/2 c. pineapple juice
1/4 c. honey
1 t. molasses
1 medium bell pepper
1 T. white bean flour
2 T. white vinegar
1 T. soy sauce
1/4 t. ground ginger

Finely chop bell pepper and simmer until tender in pineapple juice, molasses and honey. Mix remaining ingredients and add to juice mixture, stirring until thickened, about 1 minute.

Makes 1 1/2 cups.

VEGETABLE PASTA SAUCE

1 c. chopped onions
2 cloves garlic, minced
2 T. olive oil (opt.)
1 T. vegetable bouillon or salt to taste
3 c. cooked tomatoes and juice
2 c. tomato sauce
1 t. each oregano, basil, rosemary, white bean flour
1 lb. fresh or frozen mixed veggies (any kind)

In large saucepan, combine all ingredients except veggies; bring to a boil. Simmer, uncovered, for 10 minutes. Add veggies and cook an additional 5-10 minutes. Serve over hot pasta or rice. Serves 8.

TOMATO-BASIL SAUCE

2 c. tomato sauce
1 T. garbanzo bean flour
4 t. chopped parsley
1/4 t. garlic powder
1 t. ea. basil, oregano
1 t. chicken or vegetable soup base
dash white pepper

Combine all ingredients and simmer 5 minutes.

Good over enchiladas, pasta, patties, and as a pizza sauce.

SPICY RED SAUCE

This recipe does not contain beans, but is delicious over patties and loaves.

1/4 c. catsup
2 T. melted honey
2 T. sesame seeds
2 T. mustard
2 t. molasses
1 T. warm water

Mix all ingredients. Refrigerate if not used immediately.

SALSA VERDE (GREEN SAUCE)

2 3/4 c. warm water
4 T. fine white bean flour
4 t. fine corn flour or masa harina
1 small sprinkle garlic powder
1/4 t. cumin
dash white pepper
2 1/2 t. chicken or vegetable soup base
2-3 T. chopped green chiles

Whisk dry ingredients into warm water. Add green chiles. Cook 2 minutes over medium-high heat, stirring. Reduce heat to medium-low, cover and cook an additional 5 minutes to blend flavors. Makes 2 1/2 cups.

Serve over enchiladas, patties, loaves, eggs or beans. Great as the sauce for a Mexican Pizza!

MEXICAN BEAN GRAVY

2 c. cool water
1 T. chicken or vegetable soup base
1/2 t. ground cumin
1/2 t. chili powder
4 T. pinto bean flour

Mix all ingredients in a small saucepan and cook over medium-high heat for 2 minutes. Blend, if desired. Serve over patties, loaves, tamales, enchiladas, corn bread. (*Note:* you could also add 1 T. green chiles or 2 T. chopped onions to this gravy.)

WHITE BEAN GRAVY

2 c. cool water
2 t. chicken or vegetable soup base
3-4 T. white bean flour

In a small saucepan, stir all ingredients together until free of lumps. Cook over medium heat 3 minutes. Blend, if desired. Makes 2 cups.

TAMALE PIE GRAVY

2 c. warm water
2 T. chili powder
1 1/2 T. cumin
3 T. kidney or pinto bean flour
3 T. fine corn flour or masa
2 t. chicken or vegetable soup base

Stir all ingredients together until lump-free, then bring to a boil in a medium saucepan. Cook 1 min. while stirring, then cover and turn heat to low.

Cook 2 min. Add salt to taste. Serve over tamales, patties, loaves, cooked beans, potatoes.

BROWN GRAVY

2 c. water
2 t. chicken or vegetable soup base
4 T. pinto bean flour
1/2 t. Kitchen Boquet
(coloring and seasoning)
pepper to taste

Mix all ingredients well and bring to a boil. Cook over medium-high heat 2 minutes.

TOPPINGS AND COATINGS

Okara, a by-product of making soy milk or tofu, is an excellent and nutritious source of fiber. Since Okara has almost no flavor, a wide variety of seasonings can be added to create tasty snacks, breading, or topping.

Try making soy milk for soups or tofu so you can have the soy pulp (Okara) to experiment with. See instructions in the section on Tofu and Okara.

HIGH PROTEIN CRUMBLY TOPPING

*1 c. dry Okara**
4 T. butter
1/2 c. wheat germ
1/4 c. oat bran
1/4 t. garlic powder
1/4 c. dry Parmesan cheese
1 t. chicken or vegetable soup base
1 t. parsley

*See Tofu and Okara section to make Okara.

Cut butter into dry ingredients, or mix with hand or electric mixer until well mixed.

Sprinkle on top of casseroles or use as a breading for patties.

ONION FLAVORED TOPPING

*1 c. moist Okara**
4 T. dry onion soup mix

*See Tofu and Okara section to make Okara.

Squeeze as much liquid as possible from Okara.

Mix with soup mix; spread onto baking sheet coated with cooking spray. Bake at 300° 10-15 minutes, until dry and crunchy.

Use to coat patties, top casseroles or loaves. (Note: This is also great as a snack.)

ANY powdered dry soup mix can be used to flavor the moist Okara. Try as many as you can find to vary the taste of toppings or snacks.

SEASONINGS

Salt-Free seasonings are a tasty alternative to plain salt. If you choose to use these seasoning blends and add salt to taste, you will find you need far less salt than usual.

All recipes in this section are Gluten-Free when made with GF seasonings.

❤COUNTRY BLEND All Purpose Seasoning

(Salt-Free)

5 t. sesame seed
5 t. red bell pepper flakes (ground)
5 t. parsley leaves
2 1/2 t. curry powder
2 1/2 t. turmeric
2 1/2 t. cumin
1 1/2 t. mustard
1 1/4 t. garlic powder
1 1/4 t. ground lemon peel
1 1/4 t. ginger
1 1/4 t. paprika
1 1/4 t. sage
1 1/4 t. tarragon
1 t. marjoram
1 t. celery seed (ground)
1/2 t. allspice
1/2 t. ground coriander
1/2 t. rosemary
1/2 t. oregano
1/2 t. basil
1/2 t. dill weed

Optional: 3 T. dry parmesan cheese or 2 T. powdered or granular beef, chicken or vegetable soup base.

Mix well and store in air-tight jar or container.

❤COUNTRY BLEND Salt-Free Mexican (Mild)

6 T. cumin
3 T. red bell pepper, ground
3 T. paprika
3 T. oregano leaf
5 t. onion powder
1 1/4 t. garlic powder

Options: Add 3 T. parmesan cheese. For **HOT Salt-Free Mexican**, substitute 1 t. cayenne pepper for red bell pepper.

Mix well and store in air-tight jar or container.

❤COUNTRY BLEND Lentil Soup Seasoning

5 T. salt
4 t. black pepper
5 t. onion powder
3 T. parsley flakes
5 t. paprika
1 t. ground celery seed

Mix well and store in air-tight jar or container. Can be used to flavor patties, loaves, or lentil soup. (See Spicy Lentil Soup recipe on p. 87)

❤COUNTRY BLEND Vegetable Seasoning

(Salt-Free)

10 t. parsley flakes
20 t. toasted sesame seeds
5 t. red bell pepper flakes (ground)
1 1/4 t. granulated lemon peel
1 1/4 t. onion powder
1/4 t. garlic powder
1 1/4 t. paprika
2 t. crushed basil leaves
1/2 t. white pepper
1 1/4 t. ground celery seed
1 1/4 t. powdered oregano
1 t. powdered thyme
1/2 t. curry powder
1 t. ground cumin

**If desired, add 1 T. salt or 2 T. powdered vegetarian chicken broth.*

Mix well and store in air-tight jar or container.

❤COUNTRY BLEND Spicy Continental Seasoning

2 1/2 t. coarsely ground pepper
1 1/4 t. coarse or sea salt
5 t. parsley leaves, crushed
5 t. oregano leaves, crushed
2 1/2 t. paprika
1/3 t. tarragon leaves, crushed
1/3 t. ground rosemary leaves
1/2 t. celery seed, ground
1 1/4 t. lemon peel, powdered
1/3 t. garlic powder

Mix well and store in air-tight jar or container.

❤COUNTRY BLEND Popcorn Seasoning

1 T. salt
2 t. paprika
1/2 t. onion powder
1/4 t. garlic powder
1/4 t. celery seed, ground
1/2 t. lemon peel, powdered
2 t. chili powder
1/8 t. cayenne pepper

Mix well and store in air-tight jar or container.

Sprinkle generously on light buttered popcorn.

❤COUNTRY BLEND Lemon Pepper

(Salt-Free)

1 T. lemon peel, powdered
2 T. black pepper
3 T. paprika
1 t. celery seed, ground
2 t. red pepper
1 T. onion powder
2 t. garlic powder

Mix well and store in air-tight jar or container.

Excellent over fish, patties, loaves, sprinkled on top of soups before serving.

PATTIES

Meatless Patties are a favorite at our house. They cook quickly and can be served plain, with cheese or a bean gravy, or can be used on a hamburger bun. Cooked patties freeze well and thaw quickly. Most can be warmed in a toaster or toaster oven.

Most recipes in this section are Gluten-Free.

BROWN RICE BURGERS

1 c. cooked brown rice
1 egg white
1/4 c. grated onion
1/4 c. grated zucchini
2 t. grated bell pepper
2 t. red lentil or white bean flour
1/2 t. salt (opt.)
dash black pepper
dash garlic powder
1 t. dried parsley

Mix all ingredients. Drop by tablespoon onto skillet coated with cooking spray and cook over medium-low heat until browned on both sides. Serve plain, or top with White Bean Gravy.

BEAN 'N RICE BURGERS

1 c. cooked kidney beans
1 c. cooked brown rice
1 1/2 c. cooked cracked oats or wheat*
1 1/2 c. bread crumbs
1 T. sesame seeds (opt.)
1 T. sunflower seeds (opt.)
2 egg whites
1/2 c. chopped onion
1/8 c. Parmesan cheese
1 T. dijon mustard
1 T.chicken-flavored bouillon

* Sold as steel-cut or Irish oats. If unavailable, use cracked wheat or bulgar.

Combine ingredients and form into patties. Brown on both sides in skillet coated with cooking spray. Makes 8 burgers.

CHEESE PATTIES

*1 c. dry curd cottage cheese**
1 envelope Lipton Onion Soup
2 eggs
1/2 c. cooked rice or cracked wheat
1/2 c. cooked mashed beans, any kind
1 c. bread or cornflake crumbs

*See *Natural* Meals In Minutes to make non-fat cottage cheese from powdered milk.

Mix all except crumbs. Shape into patties and dip in crumbs. Place in skillet coated with cooking spray and cook, covered, over medium heat until browned and set. Turn and repeat.

SUPER PROTEIN PATTIES

3 c. cooked garbanzo beans
1 c. hulled sunflower seeds
2 eggs
1/2 onion, chopped
1 T. chicken or vegetable soup base
1/4 c. dry milk powder

Breading:
2 c. bread crumbs
1 T. chopped parsley
1/4 c. fine garbanzo bean flour
1 t. chicken or vegetable soup base

Blend patty ingredients slightly or run through hand meat grinder, in batches. Or, use a small amount of bean broth or water, as necessary, in blender. *Mixture should be chunky, not smooth.* Place in a bowl and add 1 c. bread crumbs and parsley. Form into 3" patties and coat with mixture of remaining breading ingredients. Pan-fry in skillet coated with cooking spray. Serves 4.

GARBANZO-WHEAT OR RICE PATTIES

1 c. sprouted garbanzos
1/2 c. water
1 c. cooked cracked wheat or rice
1/2 t. salt (opt)
1 t. chicken or vegetable soup base
1/8 t. garlic powder
1/2 c. chopped onions
1 T. fresh parsley, chopped

Blend garbanzos and water and pour into a mixing bowl. Add remaining ingredients and mix well. Drop by tablespoonfuls onto a skillet coated with cooking spray and cook over medium heat, covered, until browned. Turn and brown other side. Serve hot or cold.

Serves 4-6. Excellent as a meat patty substitute on hamburger buns.

EGG FOO YONG

2 t. canola oil or vegetable broth
1 c. diced celery
1 c. sliced mushrooms
1/2 c. sliced water chestnuts
1 1/2 c. bean sprouts
1/2 c. cooked rice or cracked wheat
1/2 c. chopped onion
5 eggs, lightly beaten
2 t. chicken or vegetable soup base

Heat oil or broth in a skillet and sauté the celery and onion until crispy-tender. Add mushrooms, water chestnuts and bean sprouts; cook 2 minutes longer. Remove from skillet. Combine with eggs and chicken or vegetable soup base. Drop by tablespoons into hot skillet coated with cooking spray and brown lightly on both sides. Serve with hot cooked brown rice or cracked wheat.

STUPENDOUS BEAN PATTIES

2 c. cooked, slightly mashed garbanzo beans
1/2 c. chopped onion
1 T. chopped fresh parsley
1/4 c. cooked brown rice
2 eggs
1 T. chicken or vegetable soup base

Mix all ingredients well and spoon onto hot buttered skillet. Brown on both sides.

LENTIL GARBANZO PATTIES

2 c. steamed lentils
1/2 c. garbanzo bean flour
2 T. finely minced onion
1 egg
1/2 t. salt
2 T. chicken or vegetable soup base

Mix all together. Form into small patties and fry in skillet coated with cooking spray. Brown on both sides.

GARBANZO PATTIES

1 c. sprouted garbanzos
1/2 c. whole almonds
1/2 c. water
1 c. cooked brown rice
dash garlic powder
1/4 t. onion powder
1/2 t. poultry seasoning
1 t. chicken or vegetable soup base
1/2 c. chopped onions
up to 1/2 c. wheat or bean flour to thicken patty mixture

In a blender, coarsely grind garbanzos and almonds in water. Pour into a mixing bowl. Add remaining ingredients and mix well.

Drop by tablespoonfuls onto a baking sheet coated with cooking spray and bake at 350° for 10 minutes. Turn patties over and cover; bake an additional 5 minutes. OR, pan fry over medium heat in skillet coated with cooking spray.

Serves 4-6.

TACO SOYBEAN PATTIES

1 c. ground soaked soybeans
2 t. chicken or vegetable bouillon
4 t. taco seasoning
1 t. soy sauce
1 c. cooked cracked wheat
1/2 c. onion, diced
1/2 c. green pepper, diced
2 eggs
1 c. bread or cracker crumbs

Sauté ground soybeans in 1 T. oil until lightly browned. Add to all other ingredients (reserving crumbs) and mix well.

Drop by tablespoon onto plate covered with crumbs. Press flat, turning to coat both sides. Place in hot skillet coated with cooking spray. Brown on both sides.

SOYBURGERS

2 c. cooked soybeans
1 c. cooked garbanzo beans
3 c. cooked brown rice
2 T. sesame seeds
1 large onion, chopped
1 large green pepper, chopped
1/2 c. chopped celery
1 c. chopped fresh mushrooms
1 T. chicken or vegetable soup base
3 T. soy sauce
1 t. ground ginger
1 t. sesame oil
2 eggs
1/2 c. wheat or bean flour

Mash soy and garbanzo beans or put through food grinder on coarse blade. Add to cooked rice and sesame seeds.

Cook veggies in 2 T. water for 3-4 minutes, then add to bean and rice mixture. Add remaining ingredients and mix thoroughly.

Scoop 1/4 cup portions into hot skillet coated with cooking spray . Brown on both sides.

These are excellent served on a bed of cooked spinach or Napa cabbage, topped with additional soy sauce or hot mustard.

QUICK TOFU BURGER MIX

1 1/2 c. coarse brown rice flour
1/2 c. fine white bean flour
1/3 c. toasted sesame seeds
1 T. dried parsley
1/2 c. ea. garbanzo bean flour
1/2 c. medium-fine pea flour
1 T. dry minced onion
up to 1 t. salt (opt.)
1 T. Country Blend All Purpose Seasoning *(see p. 65)* *or use your favorite no-salt blend*

Mix all ingredients together. Makes 3 1/2 cups dry mix. Refrigerate and use within 3 months.

To make Tofu Burgers, combine 1 c. dry mixture with 1 lb. mashed tofu and 1/2 c. cooked cracked wheat or brown rice. Mix well until the consistency is slightly stiff, adding a little water if mixture is too dry.

Shape into 1/2" thick patties or into balls and pan fry in skillet coated with cooking spray until crisp and golden brown on both sides.

ITALIAN "MEAT" BALLS FOR SPAGHETTI

To ***1 c. Quick Tofu Burger Mix,*** add ***2 T. bottled fat-free Italian Dressing, 1/2 c. cooked brown rice, 1 c. tofu.***

Shape into 1" balls and pan-fry. Serve on spaghetti, topped with sauce.

ORIENTAL "MEAT" BALLS TO SERVE WITH SWEET AND SOUR SAUCE

Add ***1 t. ginger and either 1 T. soy sauce or 2 t. miso to 1 c. dry mix.*** Combine with ***1 c. tofu and 1/2 c. cooked brown rice.***

Shape into 1" balls and pan-fry. Add to sauce just before serving.

LOAVES

Loaves made with a base of grains and beans are excellent sources of protein without the calories or cholesterol of meat-based loaves. For faster cooking, fill muffin tins (coated with cooking spray) to the top with loaf mixture. Bake 15-20 minutes at 350°. These can be frozen for up to 3 months, then thawed in oven or microwave.

Most recipes in this section are Gluten-Free.

VERSATILE BEAN MINI-LOAVES

2 c. mashed beans- any kind
1/2 c. cooked rice
1 T. chopped onion
1 c. finely grated carrots
2 t. chicken or vegetable soup base or salt and pepper to taste
2 eggs, beaten
2 T. Picante Sauce
1 t. cumin
1 c. bread crumbs

Mix all ingredients, adding a small amount of water, if necessary, to hold mixture together. Fill muffin tins, coated with cooking spray, full and mound top slightly. Lightly cover with foil and bake at 350° for 45 minutes. Top with grated cheese 10 minutes before done, if desired. OR, serve with White Bean Gravy or Spicy Spanish Gravy. (See pp. 61 or 76) Makes 8-12 mini-loaves.

Options: Bake in loaf pan or shape into patties and pan fry.

MEXICAN BEAN PUFFS

1/2 c. chopped onions
2 eggs
1/2 c. Picante Sauce
*1/2 c. mashed pinto beans**
1/4 c. green chiles, diced
1 c. non-fat cottage or grated cheese
1 c. cooked brown rice
4 T. chopped ripe olives
1/2 t. ea. cumin, chili powder
1 T. baking powder
1 1/2 c. wheat or spelt flour
1/2-1 t. salt

Mix all ingredients. Scoop into large muffin tins coated with cooking spray, or lined with paper bake cups and bake at 375° for 25 minutes. If desired, top with an additional 1 t. chopped olives and grated cheese and return to oven until cheese melts. OR, serve with Picante Sauce or salsa.

For **MEXICAN BEAN PUFFED SQUARES**, spread mixture evenly in 9"x13" baking dish. Bake uncovered at 400° for 15-20 minutes.

*See "Instant Mashed Beans" in the Cooking Options Section.

SPANISH BEAN LOAF

1 c. cooked brown rice or millet
1 c. cooked garbanzo or soy beans
1 c. oatmeal or dry okara
1/2 t. chili powder
1/2 t. cumin
2 beaten eggs
4 t. chicken or vegetable soup base
1 c. almonds
1 c. canned tomatoes
1/4 c. chopped green chiles or salsa

Blend or grind nuts to a coarse flour. Finely chop or coarsely grind cooked beans. Combine all ingredients. Pour into a loaf pan coated with cooking spray. Cook 45 minutes at 350°F OR fill muffin tins coated with cooking spray 3/4 full and bake for 20-25 minutes. Slice and serve plain or topped with Spicy Spanish Gravy. Serves 4-6. This looks pretty when served beside or on a bed of fresh or frozen french-sliced green beans.

Spicy Spanish Gravy

2 c. warm water
4 T. pinto bean flour
2 t. chicken or vegetable soup base
2 t. chili powder or taco seas.
2 t. cumin
salt to taste (opt)

In small saucepan, blend flour into warm water. Add spices and cook over medium heat, stirring constantly until thickened, about 30 seconds. Reduce heat to low and cook 2 minutes.

ITALIAN MINI LOAVES

1 1/2 c. tomato sauce
4 T. chopped ripe olives
2 eggs
2 T. chopped green onion
2 t. white bean flour
2 t. Italian seasoning
2 t. chicken or vegetable soup base
1/8 t. garlic powder
1 1/2 c. cooked brown rice
1/2 c. grated mozzarella cheese

Reserve 1/2 c. tomato sauce, cheese and 1/2 of olives. Mix remaining ingredients and shape into 6 mini-loaves on a baking sheet coated with cooking spray . OR, press into 9"x13" baking pan coated with cooking spray.

Bake at 375° for 15-20 minutes. Mix remaining sauce and olives.

Spoon over loaves; sprinkle with cheese. Return to oven to melt.

MEXICAN MINI LOAVES

1 c. mild taco sauce
1/2 c. cooked mushroom pieces
2 T. chopped green onion
1 egg
1-2 c. grated cheese
1/2 t. each chili powder, cumin, oregano basil
3/4 c. oatmeal
*1/4 c. mashed pinto beans**
4 T. chopped ripe olives
1 c. cooked brown rice
1/2 t. vegetable or meat flavored base

*See Cooking Options Section to make "Instant" Mashed Beans.

Mix all ingredients, saving out 1/2 c. cheese and 2 T. olives.

Shape into 3 to 6 mini-loaves on a baking sheet coated with cooking spray. OR, press into 9"x13" baking pan coated with cooking spray.

Bake at 375° for 15-20 minutes. Top with remaining cheese and olives and return to oven to melt.

MINI-MOCK SALMON LOAVES

2 c. soaked ground soybeans
1/2 c. boiling water
1 6 1/2 oz. can tuna
1 egg
1/2 t. salt
1 T. chicken or vegetable soup base
1 c. bread crumbs
1/2 c. chopped green pepper
1/2 c. chopped onions
1/2 c. chopped celery
1 1/2 T. lemon juice
1 T. dry milk powder

Combine and spoon into muffin tins coated with cooking spray. Bake at 350° for 20-30 minutes, or until set.

Top with grated cheese, cheese sauce, or your favorite sauce, if desired.

For a Gluten-Free recipe, use GF bread crumbs.

❤HEARTY❤ BEAN SOUPS

Just imagine – filling, nutritious cream soups made without fat, wheat or milk. Excellent for those with food allergies, but delicious enough to serve often to the whole family <u>*and*</u> *they can be ready in only minutes!*

To make these soups in 30 minutes or less, use beans that have been prepared in one of the following ways: (See Information Section in back of book for additional information and detailed preparation instructions.)

- ❤ *commercially canned*
- ❤ *home bottled using a pressure canner (See Home Canning Sec.)*
- ❤ *cooked and stored in refrigerator up to 1 week or in 2-cup portions in zip-loc bags in the freezer up to 6 months. (Flatten and stack bags.)*
- ❤ *sprouted and stored in refrigerator up to 1 week or in 2-cup portions in zip-loc bags in the freezer up to 6 months. (Sprouted beans cook in only 20-30 minutes.)*
- ❤ *ground to a flour (****Bean flours are the stars of today* <u>*and*</u> *tomorrow! Bean, pea and lentil flour soups are the fastest and easiest soups to make, as the bean flour cooks in only 3 minutes for excellent cream soups and soup bases, sauces and gravies.)*

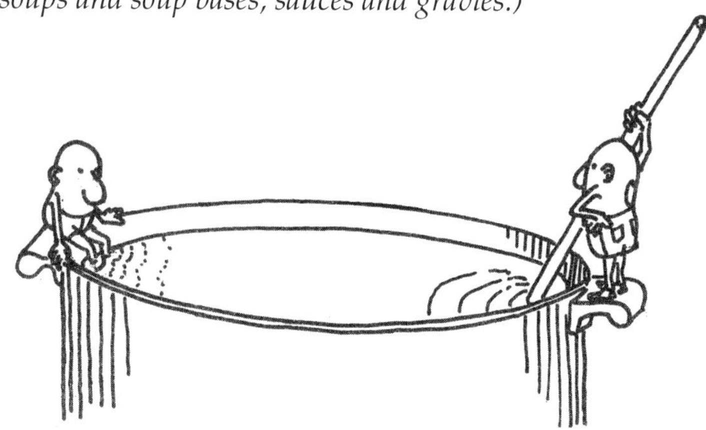

❤*All New, Unique, Revolutionary,* BEAN FLOUR for *FAST* 3-min. CREAMY BEAN SOUPS, SOUP BASES, GRAVIES OR SAUCES.

3-MINUTE BEAN FLOUR SOUPS

Use 2 T. white BEAN flour per cup of soup stock (or water and bouillon) to add flavor and color to thin soups , 3-4 T. to thicken soups, stews or gravies. Put the flour and a small amount of cool water ina plastic container and shake until free of lumps, then whisk into the boiling soup stock. Cook and stir 3 minutes. For a creamier soup, blend after cooking. For PEA and LENTIL flour soups, use only 1 T. flour per cup of liquid for thin soups, 2-3 T. for medium to thick soups.

My favorite is a "cup-a-soup" using 1 c. cool water, 1 t. "Better Than Bouillon" paste (comes in chicken, beef, mushroom, and vegetable), and 1 T. any variety of pea or lentil flour. Mix and heat to boiling, then reduce heat, cover pan and simmer 2 minutes.

For already cooked soups containing vegetables, noodles, etc.: To thicken 6 c. soup, blend 1/2 to 1 c. bean flour (depending on how thick you want the soup to be) and 2 c. cooled broth (add ice cubes to cool quickly) on high speed for 1 minute. Whisk into hot soup mixture and cook 4-5 minutes over medium high heat, stirring occasionally. Note: Blending produces a creamicr texture.

❤ **CONVENIENT REFRIGERATOR SOUPS** - Make a double batch of any of the soups in this section and ladle HOT, cooked soup into sterile quart jars, using 2-piece lids to seal. Place in refrigerator and use within one week. (Even though jar seals, preventing exchange of air, these soups should NOT be stored out of the refrigerator. Proper methods of pressure canning are the only safe way to store soups without refrigeration. See Information Section on Home Canning.)

❤ **"SOUPER" FAST NOODLE SOUPS** - Cook one package Ramen or 1 c. other dry pasta according to package directions and add 1/2-1 quart bottled soup (See Home Canning Section) and heat through.

❤ CREAMY BLENDER SOUPS without a grinder!

For **Pea or Lentil Soup**, cook 3/4 c. dry peas or lentils in 6 c. boiling water for 10 minutes. Blend 2 minutes on high. Return to pan, add 2 T. chicken soup base and cook an additional 3 minutes.

For **Creamy White Bean Soup**, cook 1 c. dry white beans in 3 c. boiling water for 20 minutes. Drain and rinse. Blend approximately 1 c. beans at a time with 2 c. hot water on high speed (8 c. water total). Repeat until all beans are blended straining out any large pieces. Return to saucepan adding 2 T. chicken or vegetable soup base and salt and pepper to taste. Cook 5 minutes over medium heat. Use as cream soup or as a creamy soup base, adding veggies in season.

3-MINUTE "CREAM OF CHICKEN" SOUP

This "practically perfect" substitute for canned Cream of Chicken soup is made without milk or fat, so can be used freely on any weight reduction diet.

4 c. boiling water
1 c. fine white bean flour
2 T. chicken or vegetable soup base
1 c. diced chicken pieces (opt.)

Mix bean flour with 2 c. cool water until free of lumps. Place water and soup base or bouillon in a medium saucepan over medium heat. Bring to a boil, then stir in bean flour mixture. Stir and cook 3 minutes. Blend for 1-2 minutes. Add chicken, if used. Serves 3-4.

CREAM OF CHICKEN SOUP SUBSTITUTE

In any recipe calling for concentrated Cream Of Chicken Soup, the following can be substituted:

1 3/4 c. cool water
5 T. white bean flour
4 t. chicken bouillon or soup base

In a medium saucepan over medium heat, bring all ingredients to a boil. Mixture will be thick in 1 minute. Reduce heat and cook over medium low for 2 more minutes.

Blend 2 minutes on high speed. Mixture thickens as it cools.

This mixture can be refrigerated up to 1 week and used in place of canned soup. Up to 1/4 c. chicken chunks can be added, if desired, after blending.

"INSTANT PEA SOUP"

1 1/2 c. boiling water
3 T. pea flour - green or yellow
2 t. chicken or vegetable soup base

Grind dried peas (whole or split) to a fine flour. (You can grind large quantities, then freeze until ready for use.) Mix pea flour with 1/2 c. cool water until free of lumps. Place water and soup base (or bouillon) in a medium saucepan over medium heat. Bring to a boil, then stir in flour mixture. Stir and cook for 1 minute. Turn heat to low, cover and cook 2 minutes. Serves 2. For a thicker soup, use up to 1/3 c. pea flour.

Note: If desired, add 1/4 c. each grated carrots, grated potatoes and minced celery to boiling water and cook 3-4 minutes or until crunchy/tender. Then, add pea flour and proceed as above.

FANTASTIC INSTANT CORN CHOWDER

2 1/4 c. hot water
1/3 c. fine corn flour or masa
3 T. pea flour
2 T. chopped pimientos
1 T. chicken or vegetable soup base
8-10 drops Tabasco sauce (opt)

Mix flours with 1 c. cool water until free of lumps. Place remaining ingredients in a medium saucepan over medium heat. Bring to a boil, then stir in flour mixture. Stir and cook for 1 minute. Cover and turn heat to low; cook 2-3 minutes. Serve with corn chips. Serves 2.

CORN AND CARROT SOUP

5 c. hot water
2 c. grated carrots
1 small tomato, diced (opt)
2 T. chopped green pepper
2 T. chicken or vegetable soup base
1/2 c. fine corn flour or masa
1/4 c. red lentil flour

In large saucepan, combine all ingredients except flours. Cook until carrots are tender, about 5-7 minutes over medium high heat. Mix flours with 1 c. cool water until smooth, then add to soup and continue cooking for 3 minutes. Serves 4.

RITA'S LENTIL SOUP

3 c. hot water
4 T. green lentil flour
2 t. lentil soup seasoning

Mix lentil flour with 1 c. cool water until free of lumps. Place hot water and seasoning in a medium saucepan over medium heat. Bring to a boil, then stir in flour mixture. Stir and cook for 1 minute. Reduce heat and cook 2 minutes. Serves 3-4.

RITA'S LENTIL SOUP SEASONING

10 T. salt
3 T. black pepper
3 T. onion powder
2 1/2 t. garlic powder
7 T. parsley flakes
3 T. paprika

Combine and store in air-tight container. Can also be used to season patties, loaves, casseroles and toppings.

CREAMY LIMA-LENTIL SOUP

2 c. hot water
3 t. chicken or vegetable bouillon
1/2 c. baby lima flour
1 T. white rice flour
1 T. red lentil flour
white pepper to taste

Stir flours into 1 c. cool water. In a medium saucepan over medium heat, whisk flour mixture into remaining ingredients. Bring to a boil, then reduce heat; cover pan and cook 2 minutes. Serves 2-3.

QUICK RED LENTIL SOUP

3 c. hot water
4 T. red lentil flour
4 t. chicken or vegetable bouillon

Stir flour into 1 c. cool water. In a medium saucepan over medium heat, whisk flour mixture into water and bouillon. Bring to a boil, then reduce heat; cover pan and cook 2 minutes. Serves 3-4.

CREAMY YELLOW PEA SOUP

3 c. hot water
4 T. yellow pea flour
4 t. chicken or vegetable bouillon
2 T. non-instant dry milk powder

Combine pea flour and milk powder and stir into 1 c. cool water. In a medium saucepan over medium heat, whisk this mixture into hot water and bouillon. Bring to a boil, then reduce heat and cook 2 minutes. Serve topped with soy "bacon bits" and chopped green onion tops. Can be blended for a richer texture. Serves 3-4.

HEARTY PINTO BEAN SOUP

3 1/2 c. water
2 c. cooked pinto beans
1 t. dry minced onions
1 T. chicken or vegetable soup base
salt and pepper to taste

Blend beans and water. Combine with remaining ingredients in a medium saucepan; heat to boiling.

Cook 3 minutes. Serves 4.

MINESTRONE SOUP

2 qt. boiling water
1 c. shredded carrots
1/4 c. finely diced onions
2 c. broken spaghetti or egg noodles
2 c. shredded potatoes
3 c. cooked kidney beans
2 T. chicken or vegetable soup base

To boiling water, add vegetables and noodles. Simmer about 10 minutes, or until noodles are tender.

Add base and beans and heat through. Serves 6.

BEAN AND BARLEY STEW

1 28 oz. can tomato or V-8 juice
1 1/2 c. water
1 c. grated carrots
1 c. finely minced celery
1 large yellow onion, chopped
1 1/2 c. cooked barley
1 c. cooked kidney beans
1 t. chicken or vegetable soup base
2-3 t. chili powder

In large saucepan, heat all ingredients to boiling. Reduce heat; cover and simmer 15 minutes.

For a thicker soup, mix 1/3 c. lentil flour with 1/2 c. water and whisk into hot soup. Cook an additional 3 minutes. Serves 6-8.

CREAMY TOMATO BASIL SOUP

4 c. boiling water
2 c. sprouted soy or small white beans
2 c. tomato sauce
1-2 T. chicken or vegetable soup base
1/4 lg. onion
1/8-1/4 t. basil

Cook beans and onion in water 15-20 minutes. Blend beans and onion in small amount of cooking water until very smooth. Pour into remaining water. Add tomato sauce and base and heat through. Serves 3-4.

BEANS 'N BARLEY SOUP

1 qt. bottled tomatoes OR
4 c. tomato juice
4 t. chicken or vegetable soup base
(use only 1 t. base if tomato juice is used)
1/2 c. dry barley
1/2 c. dry cracked beans
1/2 t. crushed basil leaves

Bring all ingredients to a boil. Reduce heat to medium and cook, covered, for 30 minutes. If desired, add 2 c. fresh, frozen or cooked veggies just before end of cooking time. Serves 3-4.

CREAMY POTATO BISQUE

7 c. boiling water
1 large onion, chopped
4 c. shredded potatoes
2 c. frozen peas
2 T. chicken or vegetable soup base
1/2 t. pepper
1/3 c. white bean flour

In large saucepan over medium-high heat, cook first 3 ingredients until potatoes are tender, about 20 minutes. Stir bean flour into 1 c. cool water, and add to soup with remaining ingredients. Cook until thick, about 1 minute, then reduce heat to low and cook, covered, for 5 minutes to blend flavors. Serve topped with fresh parsley. Serves 4-6.

CREAM OF SPINACH SOUP

1 qt. boiling water
3 c. sprouted white beans
1/4 c. frozen spinach
4 t. chicken or vegetable soup base

Cook beans in water 20 minutes. Blend beans with water to cover 3 minutes or until very creamy and smooth. Return to cooking pan, add chicken or vegetable soup base and heat through. Serves 4.

BEST CREAMY CORN CHOWDER

1 T. chicken or vegetable soup base
4 c. water
3 T. chopped onion
1 1/2 c. whole kernel corn
2 c. cooked white beans

Blend onion, corn and beans with as much water as necessary to blend very smooth. Pour into remaining water and add base. Heat through. Serve topped with a sprig of parsley and a sprinkle of celery salt and Parmesan cheese, if desired. Serves 6-8. For *Hearty Corn Chowder*, add 2 c. diced potatoes and 1 c. frozen green beans to boiling water and cook until tender. Then use cooking water to blend beans and corn. Serves 2-4.

LENTIL SOUP

1/2 to 2/3 c. red or green lentil flour
4 c. boiling water
4 t. chicken or vegetable soup base
1 lg. carrot, shredded
1 med. onion, chopped
2 ribs celery, sliced

Add all but lentil flour to 2 c. of the water and cook until crunchy/tender, about 10 minutes. Blend lentil flour with remaining water for 1 minute and add to hot soup, stirring until thick, about 1 minute. Reduce heat and cook for an additional 2 minutes. For Cream of Lentil Soup, add 1/2 c. non-instant dry milk powder while blending. Top with grated jack cheese, if desired.

Serves 3-4.

SPICY LENTIL SOUP

1 c. warm water
1 c. tomato juice
2 t. chicken or vegetable bouillon
3 T. green lentil flour
dash garlic powder
1/4 t. dried basil leaves
1 T. minced celery
2 T. minced fresh onions
white pepper to taste

In a medium saucepan over medium-high heat, bring liquids to a boil. Mix remaining ingredients into 1 c. cool water until smooth. Add to boiling liquids. Reduce heat to medium-low, cover pan and cook 2 minutes. Serves 2-3.

HOT AND SOUR SOUP

3 c. warm water seasoned with
1 Knorr Vegetable Bouillon cube
OR 1 T. chicken bouillon
2 T. white bean flour
1 1/2 t. cornstarch in 1/4 c. warm water
1/4 c. tomato or V-8 juice
1 T. chopped tomato
1 T. chopped green onions
2 T. fresh or 1 T. dehydrated mushrooms
1 T. minced celery
1 T. honey
1/2 t. Kitchen Bouquet (opt.)
1/8 t. powdered ginger
1-2 dashes white pepper to taste
2 t. soy sauce
1 t. cider vinegar
1/4 t. sesame oil

Bring all ingredients to a boil over medium-high heat and cook 1 minute. Reduce heat to low. Simmer, stirring occasionally, 5 minutes.

Note: **For EGG DROP SOUP**, quickly stir one egg into hot soup with a fork (in one direction only) until long threads form.

Serves 2-4.

BLACK BEAN SOUP

3 c. boiling water
1 clove garlic, minced
2 ribs celery, finely chopped
1 lg. carrot, finely chopped
1 c. chopped cabbage
1 lg. onion, finely chopped
1/8 t. cayenne pepper
4 c. cooked black beans
2 c. hot cooked brown rice
salt and pepper to taste

Combine all but beans and rice; cook until veggies are crunchy/tender, about 5 minutes. Add beans and thicken, if desired. Place 1/2 c. hot rice in each bowl, then top with soup. (Note: For an extra hot flavor, pass the Tabasco Sauce and allow each person to"hotten" up his own soup.) Serves 4-6.

BLACK BEAN AND TOMATO SOUP

4 c. boiling water
1 c. diced onion
1/2 c. diced green pepper
6 c. cooked black beans
1/4 t. pepper (opt)
1 1/2 T. vegetable soup base
1 c. tomato sauce
dash cumin

In a large cooking pot, combine water and vegetables; cook over medium heat for 5-10 minutes. Add remaining ingredients and heat through. Serves 8. This soup is excellent when served over hot, cooked brown rice.

MANY BEAN SOUP

4 c. boiling water or tomato juice
1 c. each chopped onion, celery, carrots, potatoes, cabbage
1/8 t. garlic powder
Pepper to taste (opt)
4 c. any combination cooked beans
1 T. vegetable soup base (use only 1 t. base if tomato juice is used)

Combine water and fresh vegetables and cook until tender. Add remaining ingredients and heat through. Serves 6.

HARVEST SPECIAL

4 c. boiling water
1 c. finely chopped onion
1/2 c. chopped bell pepper
2 c. red kidney beans, cooked
2 c. lima beans, cooked
2 c. chopped zucchini
1 c. chopped mushrooms
2 c. fresh or frozen corn
1 t. Worcestershire sauce
1 T. chicken or vegetable soup base
1 c. Jack cheese, grated (opt)

Combine water and all fresh vegetables and cook over medium heat for 10 minutes, or until veggies are crunchy/tender. Add remaining ingredients, except cheese and heat through. Serve topped with Jack cheese. Serves 6-8.

MACARONI SOUP

2 qt. boiling water
1 c. shell macaroni
2 T. chicken or vegetable soup base
2 c. cooked garbanzo beans
1 c. ea. chopped carrots, onion, celery, spinach, mushrooms, zucchini

Add all but cooked beans to boiling water and cook over medium heat for 10-15 minutes, or until macaroni is tender. Add cooked beans and simmer 5 minutes more. Serve topped with Parmesan cheese. Serves 4-6.

SHEEPHERDER'S HEARTY SOUP

1/2 c. chopped celery
1/4 c. diced onion
1 c. water
2 T. white bean flour
1/3 c. dry milk powder
3 c. cooked lima beans
2 c. cooked whole kernel corn
1 c. cooked tomatoes, chopped
1/2 c. shredded Jack cheese
vegetable seasoning salt to taste
Dash of hot pepper sauce

Combine water and raw veggies and cook 8 minutes, or until tender. Mix flour and dry milk powder with 1 c. cool water, then whisk into hot soup. Add remaining ingredients. Heat thoroughly, but do not boil. Season to taste with salt, pepper and hot sauce. Serve with wedges of sheepherder's or sour dough bread. Serves 6-8.

TOMATO-BEAN SOUP

1/2 c. chopped green bell pepper
1/4 c. chopped onion
1/8 t. garlic powder
4 c. cooked kidney beans
6 c. canned tomatoes, undrained, cut into pieces
1 c. shredded cheddar cheese
2 c. water
1 1/2 c. tomato juice
1 c. fresh or frozen corn
1 T. chili powder
1 t. cumin
2 T. chicken or vegetable soup base

In 4 qt. saucepan or Dutch oven, combine all ingredients except cheese. Bring to a boil over medium-high heat. Reduce heat; simmer 10 minutes, stirring occasionally. Sprinkle each serving with 2 T. of the shredded cheese. Serves 6-8.

CREAM OF ASPARAGUS SOUP

6 c. hot water
1 t. salt
1/8 t. white pepper
1/4 t. onion powder
1/8 t. turmeric
1 c. cut asparagus stems
1 c. white bean flour
1 c. milk (optional)

Bring all ingredients to a boil and cook 3 minutes, then blend 1 minute, in small batches. Strain to remove tough asparagus pieces. Return to pan and cook an additional 1 minute. If desired, top with grated cheese and chopped parsley. *Note:* Six chicken or vegetable bouillon cubes can be used instead of seasonings. Add pepper to taste. Serves 4-6.

CLAM AND BEAN CHOWDER

2 qt. boiling water
1 medium onion, chopped
6 c. shredded potatoes
2 c. sliced celery
2 c. thinly sliced carrots
2 c. cooked white beans
1 1/2 c. dry milk powder
1 T. chicken or vegetable soup base
2 T. clam base OR 2 small cans minced clams
1/8 t. pepper
salt to taste

Sprinkle milk powder and base over vegetables and mix well. Add to boiling water while stirring. Cook for 10 minutes, or just until vegetables are tender. Thicken, if desired, with cornstarch or flour. Serves 10-12.

BEAN AND MUSHROOM SOUP

1 1/2 c. chopped onions
1 c. thinly sliced carrots
1/2 lb. mushrooms, sliced
3 c. boiling water
1/4 c. chopped parsley
1 c. cooked white beans
1/4 t. black pepper
4 t. chicken or vegetable soup base

Combine all ingredients and cook 15 minutes over medium-high heat. Blend 1/2 of mixture until smooth and return to pan. Serve hot. (This soup is even better after a day or two, so make a large batch and refrigerate leftovers for "Sooper" Quick lunches.) Serves 4.

RED AND WHITE POTATO SOUP

7 c. boiling water
2 c. shredded potatoes
1/2 c. finely chopped celery
1 t. dried parsley
3 T. chicken or vegetable soup base
1/2 c. finely chopped onion
1 c. cooked kidney beans
1/2 c. white bean flour

Combine all ingredients except bean flour. Cook over medium high heat about 15 minutes until potatoes are tender. Stir bean flour into 1 c. cool water until free of lumps, then into hot mixture. Cook an additional 3 minutes. Serves 6-8.

CLAMLESS CHOWDER

7 c. boiling water
2 c. shredded potatoes
1 c. shredded onions
1 1/2 c. shredded carrots
1 c. clam juice
1/2 c. white bean flour
2 c. cooked lima beans

Combine all but cooked beans and flour; cook over medium high heat 15 minutes, or until tender.

Stir bean flour into 1 c. cool water, then whisk into hot soup; add lima beans and cook an additional 5 minutes. Serves 6-8.

CREAMY CABBAGE SOUP

3 c. boiling water
1/2 c. finely chopped onion
1 1/2 T. chicken or vegetable soup base
2 c. shredded cabbage
1/3 c. white bean flour

Combine all but bean flour. Cook over medium high heat for 15 minutes. Stir bean flour into 1 c. cool water, then whisk into hot soup; cook an additional 3 minutes. Serves 4-6.

SPROUTED LENTIL SOUP

7 c. boiling water
1 diced green pepper
2 c. bottled tomatoes
1 lg. chopped onion
4 lg. grated carrots
1 T. chicken or vegetable soup base
2 c. sprouted lentils
1/2 c. white bean flour

Combine all but bean flour; bring to a boil, then turn to medium and cook 15 minutes, until carrots are tender. Stir bean flour into 1 c. cool water, then whisk into hot soup; cook an additional 3 minutes.

SURPRISINGLY YUMMY SPICY LENTIL STEW

1 lb. dry lentils
5 c. water
2 medium onions, diced
1 T. chicken or vegetable soup base
2 c. tomato sauce
1 small bay leaf
1 t. liquid smoke flavoring
2 c. tomato juice
3 T. molasses
2 T. barbecue sauce
1/8 t. each garlic powder, dry mustard, cinnamon, cloves, ginger, nutmeg, dried savory, thyme

In large pan, combine lentils, 5 c. water and seasonings. Bring to a boil; reduce heat and cook, covered for 30 minutes. Add remaining ingredients and simmer, covered 15 minutes. Remove bay leaf. Freezes well. Serves 8.

CREAMY BROCCOLI SOUP

4 c. chopped broccoli
1/2 c. chopped onion
3 c. boiling water
1 c. chopped celery
2 T. chicken or vegetable soup base
1/2 t. basil leaves
dash garlic powder
1/3 c. white bean flour

In large saucepan, combine all but bean flour. Bring to a boil, then reduce heat and simmer covered 15 minutes or until broccoli is tender. Blend 1/3 of soup mixture and bean flour at a time until smooth. Return to pan and cook an additional 5 minutes. Serves 3-4.

FRESH VEGETABLE SOUP

4 c. boiling water
4 t. chicken or vegetable soup base
1/2 t. basil leaves
1/8 t. pepper
1 clove garlic, minced
1/2 c. diced onion
1 c. grated carrot
2 c. grated zucchini
1 c. chopped tomato
2 t. chopped parsley
3 c. cooked red beans

In large saucepan, combine all ingredients except beans. Bring to a boil; reduce heat and simmer, covered, 15 minutes. Blend 1/2 of soup mixture. Add beans and cook an additional 5 minutes. For variety, substitute tomato juice or V-8 for water and add only 1 t. chicken or vegetable soup base. Serves 6.

NOODLE-BEAN SOUP

1 lb. pasta noodles, any kind
8 c. boiling water
3 T. chicken or vegetable soup base
1/2 c. chopped green onions
2 c. white beans, cooked
2 c. fresh or frozen corn
2 c. kidney beans, cooked
2 c. fresh or frozen peas

In large saucepan, combine water and noodles. Bring back to a boil. Reduce heat to low; cook 15 minutes, stirring occasionally. Add remaining ingredients and cook over medium heat 10 minutes. Serves 6.

MUSHROOM BARLEY SOUP

1 c. dry barley
5 c. boiling water
1 T. chicken or vegetable soup base
1 bay leaf
2 onions, chopped
2 stalks thinly sliced celery
1 c. sliced mushrooms
1/4 t. pepper
1 c. cooked pink beans

Add barley to boiling water and cook, covered, 10 minutes. Add remaining ingredients except beans and cook over low heat 20 minutes, or until barley is tender Add pink beans and heat through. Remove bay leaf before serving. Serves 4-6.

HEARTY RICE SOUP

4 c. boiling water
1 c. cooked brown rice
1 c. cooked blackeyes
1 large clove garlic, minced
1 T. dried parsley
1 T. soy sauce
1/4 c. minced parsley tops
1/2 c. onion, finely chopped
1 c. chopped tomatoes
4 t. chicken or vegetable soup base
1/4 t. ginger
white pepper to taste
2 c. any kind cooked vegetables (fresh, frozen or leftovers)

Combine all ingredients and bring to a boil. Reduce heat and simmer 10 minutes. Serve with toasted wheat bread or crackers. Serves 5.

CLAIR'S ORIENTAL RICE SOUP

7 c. water
2 T. white bean flour
2 T. chicken or vegetable soup base
1 t. ginger
dash (or two) white pepper
4 t. honey
2 T. soy sauce
3 T. sweet and sour sauce or oriental oyster sauce
1 lg. onion, cut in 1" chunks
2 c. chicken-flavored gluten, cut into very thin strips (or use tofu)*
4 c. hot, cooked brown rice

(*see The Amazing Wheat Book by LeArta Moulton.)
Bring water to a boil; whisk in all ingredients except rice and gluten or tofu. Simmer, covered, until onions are crunchy/tender, about 4 minutes. Add gluten or tofu and heat through. Serve in bowls over hot cooked rice. Serves 6.

SAVORY BEAN STEW

4 c. boiling water
2 c. diced potatoes
1 c. diced carrots
1 c. diced onions
2 c. fresh or frozen green beans
1/2 t. Worcestershire sauce
1 qt. bottled tomatoes
1 T. chicken or vegetable soup base
1/2 c. cooked brown rice or barley
1 c. cooked pinto beans
2 c. cooked soy beans
salt and pepper to taste

Bring all ingredients to a boil; reduce heat to medium and cook, covered for 15-20 minutes. Thicken, if desired with pea, barley or bean flour. Serves 8.

ORIENTAL VEGETABLE SOUP

4 c. boiling water
4 T. chicken or vegetable soup base
1/2 t. ground ginger
1 c. sliced fresh mushrooms
1 T. soy sauce
1 c. chopped celery
1 c. chopped onion
1 c. chopped green pepper
1 c. cooked brown rice
1 c. Napa cabbage
1 c. cooked white beans

Add all except rice, cabbage and beans and bring to a boil. Reduce heat and cook, covered for 10 minutes. Add cabbage and rice; cook 5 minutes. Serve with extra soy sauce, if desired. Serves 6-8.

BLACK BEAN SOUP AND SALAD

2 c. boiling water
1 c. tomato juice
2 onions, chopped
2 cloves garlic, minced
1 t. cumin
1 t. oregano
2 T. chicken or vegetable soup base
2 T. vinegar
2 T. lemon juice
1/2 t. molasses
dash cayenne pepper, or to taste
6 c. cooked black beans

In a large saucepan, bring all ingredients except beans to a boil. Reduce heat and cook over medium-high heat for 5 minutes, until onions are tender. Add cooked beans and heat through. Serve topped with a choice of salad-bar toppings such as chopped tomatoes, green pepper, chopped egg, chopped olives, sliced celery, or grated cheese. Serves 8.

HOT PEPPER BEAN SOUP

3 c. boiling water
1 c. chopped onions
1 small hot pepper, chopped
2 c. sliced carrots
1/2 t. garlic powder
1 T. chicken or vegetable soup base
2 t. chicken or vegetable soup base
dash Tabasco sauce
3 c. hot cooked rice
6 c. cooked black beans

To boiling water, add all but beans and rice. Cook 7-10 minutes, until veggies are tender. Add beans and heat through, adding more base to taste if beans and rice were cooked without salt. Ladle into serving bowls and top with mounds of rice. Serves 6-8.

FIESTA SOUP

4 c. boiling water
4 t. chicken or vegetable soup base
1 medium onion, diced
1 c. cooked kidney beans
1 c. sliced cauliflower
1 c. grated carrots
1 c. grated zucchini
2 c. fresh or frozen green beans
1 T. parsley
1 t. chopped basil

Bring all ingredients to a boil. Cover and reduce heat to medium; cook 15 minutes. Thicken, if desired. Serves 4-6.

ASPARAGUS NOODLE SOUP

4 c. boiling water
1 T. chicken or vegetable soup base
2 c. broken spaghetti pieces
1/2 t. paprika
2 c. chopped asparagus (tough ends)
1 t. chopped parsley
1 c. chopped celery
1 c. cooked soybeans

Bring water, chicken or vegetable soup base and asparagus ends to a boil and cook, covered, 5 mins. Blend with part of the cooking water for 2 minutes and strain out pulp. Pour liquid back into boiling water and add remaining ingredients.

Bring back to a boil and cook, stirring occasionally 10-15 minutes. Thicken if desired. Add vegetable seasoning to taste. Serves 4-6.

BARLEY LIMA SOUP

4 c. boiling water
1/2 c. barley
1 T. parsley flakes
2 T. chicken or vegetable soup base
1 c. chopped cabbage
1 c. chopped celery
1 c. chopped onion
1 c. chopped potatoes
1 c. cooked lima beans

Bring barley and water to a boil; cook 15 minutes. Add remaining ingredients and cook another 15 minutes, or just until veggies are tender. Add vegetable seasoning or salt to taste.

TAMALE SOUP

4 c. boiling water
1 c. fresh or frozen cut corn
1 T. chicken or vegetable soup base
1 qt. bottled tomatoes
1 c. chopped green onions
3/4 c. chopped green pepper
1 c. cooked brown rice
1 t. chili powder
1 t. cumin
1 c. chopped ripe olives
2 c. grated cheddar cheese

Add all but olives and cheese to boiling water. Bring back to a boil; cook, covered over medium heat for 15 minutes. Top individual bowls with olives and grated cheese. Serves 6. (Great with buttered corn bread.)

CREAMY SOY SOUP

4 c. soy milk
1 t. fresh or dried parsley
1 T. chicken or vegetable soup base
1/4 c. white bean flour
1/2 c. grated white cheese

Slowly heat all but cheese and bean flour. When hot, whisk in bean flour mixed with 1/2 c. cool water, and cook an additional 3 minutes. Ladle into bowls and top with grated cheese and extra parsley, if desired. This is also an excellent soup base. Add cooked vegetables, pasta, beans or grains. This is also excellent as a cold soup. Serves 4.

To make soy milk, blend 1 c. soaked soybeans with 3 c. ***boiling*** water for 2-3 minutes (do this in 2 batches). Strain milk and save pulp to use in baking or dry for casserole toppings. Coat a large saucepan with baking spray and cook over medium-low heat for 8-10 minutes. Stir occasionally to prevent a film from forming on top. *For drinking,* add 1/2 t. oil (opt.) and 1-2 t. honey to each cup.

RED LENTIL SOUP

6 c. boiling water
1/2 c. red lentil flour
1/2 c. white bean flour
2 T. chicken or vegetable soup base
2 medium potatoes, cubed
1/2 onion, diced
1 c. diced chicken pieces (opt.)
1/4 c. dry milk powder (opt.)

Stir flours into 2 c. cool water until free of lumps. In a large, heavy saucepan, combine with remaining water and cook over medium-high heat for 3 minutes, stirring occasionally. Blend 2 minutes, until smooth. Add dry milk powder while blending, if used. Return to pan and add remaining ingredients. Cook over medium-low heat for 15 minutes, stirring occasionally. Garnish with parsley, chives, or grated white cheese. Serves 6.

TOMATO BASIL SPROUT SOUP

4 c. water
2 c. sprouted soybeans
2 c. sprouted garbanzo beans
1 c. sprouted pinto beans

Pressure cook 5 minutes at 15 lb. pressure, or cook until tender over medium-high heat, about 20 minutes. Add:

1 c. fresh or frozen corn
1 qt. bottled tomatoes, chopped
1 t. basil
2 T. chicken or vegetable soup base
1/8 t. pepper

Cook 5-10 minutes more. If a thicker soup is desired, add 4 T. cornstarch or 8 T. white bean flour to 1/2 c. warm water and stir into hot soup. Cook an additional 3 minutes. Serves 6.

HEARTY RED BEANS AND RICE SOUP

1 c. cooked brown rice
1 c. cooked red beans
4 c. boiling water
1 T. dried parsley
1 T. soy sauce
1/2 c. onion, finely chopped
1 c. chopped tomatoes
1 T. chicken or vegetable soup base
1/4 t. ginger
Tabasco sauce to taste
2 c. any kind cooked vegetables (fresh, frozen, or leftovers)

Mix all ingredients together; bring to a boil over high heat. Reduce heat to low and cook 10 minutes. Serve with toasted wheat bread or crackers. Serves 4-6.

ALPHABET SOUP MIX

2 c. dry split peas
2 c. lentils
2 c. pearl barley
1 c. dry cracked beans (any kind)
2 c. dry minced onion
3 T. parsley flakes
2 c. dry alphabet noodles

Combine ingredients and store in quart jars in a cool place. All ingredients cook in about the same amount of time. Especially good beans to try are navy, kidney, soy, garbanzo and white. Makes about 3 qt. of mix.

To make soup for 6, add 3 c. mixture to 8 c. boiling water seasoned with your choice of soup base. Cook until tender. OR, add 3 c. mix to 5 c. tomato or V-8 juice and 3 c. water and cook until tender.

PRETTY AS A PRESENT SOUP

3 c. dry red beans
2 c. dry white beans
3 c. dry black beans
4 c. alphabet noodles
3 c. split peas
2 c. dry pearl barley
1 c. dry minced onion
Seasoning packets (below)

In order given, divide ingredients equally into four wide-mouth quart jars, being careful to keep each ingredient in a separate layer. Fill jars completely to the top. Place lids on jars and top with seasoning packet.

Seasoning Packets: Cut four 6" squares plastic wrap. Onto each square, place 1 T. powdered chicken or vegetable bouillon or 3 bouillon cubes, 1/2 t. salt or vegetable seasoning, 1/2 t. ground cumin, 1/4 t. pepper, 1 t. basil, 1/8 t. ginger, 1/8 t. garlic powder. Fold in edges to form a square and place packet on top of jar lid. (You could also use commercial powdered soup seasoning mixes.)

Cover with 8" calico circle and tie twine or ribbon around outside of jar about 3/4" down.

To cook: Place 1 qt. bean mixture in a large cooking pan with 10 c. water. Bring to a boil for 2 minutes. Remove from heat, cover and let sit 1 hour. Bring back to a boil, reduce heat to medium-low and add one seasoning packet and fresh vegetables, as desired. Cook until tender, usually 15-30 minutes, adding additional water as necessary.

The idea for the seasoning packets came from an old copy of a newspaper recipe, source unknown. Note: Be sure to give cooking instructions with your gift.

CASSEROLES AND ONE-DISH MEALS

Whether you prepare in advance or at the last minute, Casseroles and One-Dish Meals provide an excellent way to serve whole or hidden beans.

With convenient home-bottled beans, frozen cooked beans, cooked beans stored in the refrigerator, or commercially canned beans from your shelf, you will be able to make a delicious, nutritious meal in 30 minutes or less.

If a recipe calls for cooked, mashed beans, see the Cooking Options Section for "Instant Mashed Beans."

Most recipes in this section are Gluten-Free.

SOYBEAN LASAGNE

In a skillet coated with baking spray, sauté until lightly browned:
1 lg. onion, chopped
1 clove garlic, minced
2 c. coarsely ground cooked soybeans
Add and simmer for 10 min:
4 c. canned tomatoes and juice
1 6 oz. can tomato paste
1 small can chopped olives
1/4 t. pepper
1 t. salt
1 t. basil
2 c. sliced raw mushrooms
2 T. white bean flour

Layer in two 9"x13" pans alternately with:
1 lb. cooked lasagne noodles (or zucchini sliced lengthwise)
1/2 c. grated Parmesan
1 c. chopped green or yellow peppers
*1 lb. fat-free cottage cheese or ricotta**
1 c. fresh or frozen broccoli tops
*1 1/2 c. grated mozzarella**
1 c. torn spinach leaves
1 c. coarsely grated carrots
1 c. fresh or frozen cauliflower

*See *Natural* Meals In Minutes, Cheeses Section for fat-free cheeses.

Bake at 350° for 30 minutes covered, then 15 minutes uncovered, or until firm. Let cool 10 minutes before serving. Serves 8-10. Note: Freezes well. Leftovers are great for lunches and snacks.

MEXICAN BEAN BAKE

2 c. boiling water
1/2 lg. onion, grated
1/2 c. green chile salsa
6 corn tortillas, cut in fourths
1/2 c. pinto bean flour
2 c. cooked rice
1 T. chicken or vegetable soup base
1 1/2 c. grated jack cheese (opt.)

Whisk bean flour into water. Add salsa, onions and base; bring back to a boil. Cook 3 minutes over medium heat. In 1 qt. baking dish, layer rice, 1/2 tortillas and 1/2 salsa mixture. Top with tortillas and salsa mixture and cheese, if desired.

Bake at 350° until cheese bubbles, about 10-15 minutes. Cover if you omit cheese. Serves 4-6.

ORIENTAL VEGETABLES ALMONDINE

1/2 t. sesame oil
*2 T. canola oil**
2 c. mushrooms, sliced
2 c. napa cabbage
1/2 c. carrot slivers
1/2 c. chopped onion
2 c. chopped celery
2 c. warm water
1/2 c. white bean flour
2 t. chicken or vegetable soup base
2 c. chow mein noodles
1 c. chopped toasted almonds

Sauté vegetables in oil (*or omit canola oil and use 1/4 c. water to steam) until tender. Place in 9"x13" baking dish. Whisk bean flour and chicken or vegetable base into warm water. Cook 3 minutes over medium heat. Pour over vegetables. Top with noodles and almonds. Bake uncovered at 350° for 10-15 minutes.

LO MEIN

1 pkg (1 lb) flat noodles, cooked
2 c. chopped celery
6 green onions and tops, chopped
4 c. thinly sliced cabbage
2 chicken breasts, diced
OR, 1 c. cubed tofu
1-2 t. chopped garlic
1 T. chicken soup base (paste)
OR 3 chicken bouillon cubes
1/2 t. flavored sesame oil
1 T. soy sauce
1 T. ea. cornstarch , white bean flour
dissolved in 1/4 c. warm water

In heavy skillet, cook one veggie at a time in about 1/2 tsp. canola oil, or 2 T. warm water over high heat. When sizzling, add about 1/4 c. water which should create lots of steam (quickly cooks veggies). Cook 1-2 minutes, until veggies are crunchy-tender. There should not be any water left. Spoon into large serving bowl. When all veggies and meat or tofu are cooked, pour liquid into skillet, add remaining ingredients and cook just until thick. Pour over veggies, add hot cooked noodles, toss and serve.

LENTIL GARBANZO CASSEROLE

2 T. canola oil or vegetable broth
1 small onion, chopped
1 c. cooked brown rice
1 c. cooked lentils
3/4 c. cooked garbanzos
1 c. boiling water
4 t. chicken or vegetable soup base
1 T. parsley flakes
1/4 c. fine corn flour

Brown onion in oil or broth. Add remaining ingredients and mix well. Turn into an 8" square casserole dish coated with cooking spray and bake at 350° for 25 minutes. If desired, top with cheese or buttered bread crumbs. Serves 3-4.

QUICK SKILLET QUICHE

1 3/4 c. cooked brown rice
2 T. chopped olives
1 T. chopped green onions
2 T. chopped onion
1/4 c. fresh sliced mushrooms
1/2 c. yogurt
1 c. cottage cheese
2 t. chicken or vegetable soup base
2 T. Picante sauce
3 eggs

Mix and pour into 10" skillet coated with cooking spray. Top with 1 c. grated mild cheese, if desired. Cover and cook over medium-low heat until center is nearly set or cheese is melted. Cut into wedges and serve hot. Serves 4-6.

CREAMY CHICKEN DOUBLE BEAN CASSEROLE

2 c. cooked brown rice
2 c. cooked black beans
4 c. boiling water
1/2 t. salt
1/8 t. pepper
1 1/2 T. parsley flakes
2 T. grated onion
1/8 t. thyme
scant t. basil
5 t. chicken or vegetable soup base
2/3 c. white bean flour

Layer cooked rice, then beans in 9"x13" baking dish. Whisk remaining ingredients into boiling water. Bring to a boil, then cook 3 minutes over medium heat. Pour over rice and beans. Cover and bake 15-20 minutes until heated through. OR, top with corn flakes, cracker or bread crumbs and bake uncovered.

Serves 4-6.

CREAMY 4-VEGETABLE CASSEROLE

3 c. shredded potatoes
1 c. shredded cabbage
2 c. shredded carrots
1 c. beans, any kind
2 eggs
5 T. chopped chives, divided
1 T. chicken or vegetable soup base
1/4 t. pepper
1 c. yogurt or sour cream

In medium saucepan, cook potatoes, cabbage and carrots in 1 c. water until tender, about 8-10 minutes. Add additional water if necessary to prevent sticking.

Drain and blend vegetables, using only enough cooking water to make a thick puree. (Some chunks are O.K.) Add remaining ingredients, reserving sour cream and 1 T. chives. Spread in 1 1/2 qt. shallow baking dish. Bake in a 350° oven 15 minutes.

In small bowl, mix sour cream and chives; spread over vegetables. Bake 5 minutes longer. Serves 6-8.

2-BEAN SKILLET SUPPER

1 c. diced tomatoes
1 c. thinly sliced celery
1/4 c. diced green pepper
1 c. water or tomato juice
1 T. white bean flour
2 c. cooked lima beans
1-2 t. chicken or vegetable soup base
1 c. frozen green beans

Sauté or steam raw vegetables until crunchy/tender. Add liquid mixed with bean flour and bring to a boil to thicken.

Add remaining ingredients and heat through. Serve over hot brown rice or in bowls with corn bread.

Serves 4-6.

DOUBLE CHEESY TACOS OR TORTILLAS

1/2 c. cooked brown rice or cracked wheat
3/4 c. cooked red beans
1/4 t. cumin
1/2 c. chopped onions
1 T. chopped green chiles
1 T. parmesan cheese
1/2 c. cottage cheese
salt to taste
4-6 flour tortillas or taco shells
shredded lettuce and chopped tomatoes

Heat all ingredients. Fill heated tortillas or taco shells. Top with lettuce and tomatoes.

Serves 4-6.

MAGIC CRUST TACO PIE

1 1/3 c. yogurt cottage cheese
or 1 c. grated cheddar cheese
2 c. cooked kidney beans
1 c. cooked brown rice or cracked wheat
1/2 c. chopped fresh onions
3 eggs
1 c. water
1 T. oil (opt.)
2 T. diced green chiles
2 t. cumin
1 t. chili powder
1/3 c. dry milk powder
1/3 c. white bean flour
1/3 c. cornmeal
1 can (4 1/2 oz.) chopped ripe olives
4 t. chicken or vegetable soup base

Coat a 9"x13" baking dish with cooking spray. Layer with cheese, beans, wheat and onions.

Blend remaining ingredients (except olives) for 1 min. Pour over beans. Top with olives.

Bake at 350° 20-30 minutes, until firm. Serves 6.

BEANCHILADAS

8 Whole Wheat Flour Tortillas
2 c. grated cheese (Opt.)

Sauce:

2 T. fine white bean flour
1 T. chili powder
1 T. ground cumin
2 c. water or bean juice
1/2 t. oregano
2 t. chicken or vegetable soup base

Filling:

2 c. mashed kidney or pinto beans
1/4 c. chopped onion
1/4 c. chopped green onion
1 c. cottage cheese
1/2 c. chopped green pepper
1/2 c. oatmeal
1/2 c. chopped black olives
2 T. yogurt
2 t. chicken or vegetable soup base

Combine sauce ingredients and cook over medium heat for 5 minutes. Mix filling ingredients. Dip tortillas in sauce, then place filling in sauce in middle, roll and place seam side down in shallow baking dish. Pour remaining sauce over all.

Top with grated cheese, if used. Bake, covered at 350° for 15 minutes, basting occasionally with sauce. Uncover and cook 5 more minutes.

FREEZER BEAN BURRITOS

24 Whole Wheat Flour Tortillas
Filling from Beanchiladas
1 c. cooked rice or cracked wheat
1/2 c. mild Picante Sauce
1/2 c. chopped green chiles
2 c. grated cheese

Combine all ingredients except tortillas. Fill each flour tortilla with 1/4 c. of mixture.

Roll up, folding in edges, and wrap individually in foil or plastic wrap. When ready to serve, thaw, unwrap, place in baking pan, and bake, covered, at 400° for 30 minutes.

Serve on a bed of lettuce. Top with additional lettuce and chopped tomatoes. (For 6 servings, use 3 cups lettuce and 2 c. tomatoes.)

BLACK BEAN BURRITOS (Our Favorite!)

6 flour tortillas
2 1/2 c. refried beans made with black bean flour (see p. 123)
1/2 c. Picante Sauce or Salsa Verde (see p. 60)
1/2 c. chopped fresh onions (white or green)
2 c. low or no-fat cottage cheese (opt.)

Spread each tortilla with 1/3 c. cooked refried bean mix. Top with remaining ingredients. Roll and place in covered baking dish. Microwave 2-3 minutes, or bake at 350° 15 minutes.

Note: This recipe can be made with black, pinto or any red bean flour.

To freeze, make a double or triple batch and wrap filled tortillas in foil or plastic wrap. Thaw, then bake as directed above. (Great for after school snacks!)

BLACK BEAN TACO PIZZAS

Following the above directions for Black Bean Burritos, lay tortillas on baking sheet, then layer ingredients as for pizza. Broil until bubbly, then top with ***fresh chopped tomatoes, chopped olives, shredded lettuce and additional salsa.*** Serve hot.

LIZZY'S EASY ENCHILADAS

1 c. chopped onions
1/2 t. oregano
2 T. chili powder
1 T. chicken or vegetable bouillon OR, salt to taste
3 1/2 c. water
3/4 c. pinto bean flour
1 c. tomato sauce
2 c. cooked red or pinto beans
1/4 t. tabasco sauce (opt)
12 corn tortillas
2 c. mozzarella or jack cheese, grated

Simmer onions, tomato sauce and seasonings in water 3 minutes. Whisk in bean flour and cook 1 minute.

Add cooked beans and hot sauce, then layer sauce, tortillas and cheese (repeating until ingredients are used up), in 9"x13" pan.

Bake at 400° 15-20 minutes. Serves 8-10.

BEAN AND RICE BURRITOS

6-8 flour tortillas
1 c. refried beans (see p. 123)
1 c. grated cheese (opt.)
1 c. cooked brown rice
1/4 c. chopped ripe olives
1/2 c. chopped green onions
1/4-1/2 c. Picante or Enchilada sauce
1/4 c. tomato sauce

Mix well. Divide filling into tortillas, roll and heat to eat, or freeze.

Can be served plain or with sauce or cheese. Serves 6-8.

LAYERED BURRITO CASSEROLE

Using the Burrito recipe above, or Black Bean Burritos on p. 107, layer ingredients in a 9" casserole dish.

Top with additional grated or cottage cheese and bake 15 minutes at 350° or until bubbly.

TOFU PEPPER STIR FRY

4 c. celery, sliced diagonally
1 green sweet pepper, sliced
1 red sweet pepper, sliced
1/2 pound fresh mushrooms, sliced
1/2 t. finely minced garlic
1/2 c. yellow onions, sliced
1 c. fresh mung or soy bean sprouts
1 c. frozen, then thawed tofu, cubed

Sauce:

2 c. warm water
2 t. chicken or vegetable bouillon
3 T. soy sauce
1/2 t. powdered ginger
white pepper to taste
2 T. cornstarch
4 t. white bean flour

Marinate tofu (after all water has been squeezed out) in sauce ingredients while stir-frying veggies. Then press out all liquid and stir-fry tofu in skillet coated with cooking spray.

In heavy skillet, cook one veggie at a time in about 1/2 tsp. vegetable oil or 2 T. water over high heat. When sizzling, add about 1/4 c. water which should create lots of steam (quickly cooks veggies). Cook 1-2 minutes, until veggies are crunchy-tender. There should not be any water left. Spoon into large serving bowl. Cook sauce liquid squeezed from tofu 3 minutes. Pour over veggies and tofu and serve over hot cooked brown rice.

MILLET AND BEAN CASSEROLE

1 c. cooked millet or brown rice
1 c. cooked lima beans
1 T. chicken or vegetable soup base
1 lg. onion, chopped
1 clove garlic, minced
1/2 c. finely grated carrots
2 c. tomato sauce
1 1/2 c. oatmeal
2 t. dry sweet basil
1/4 t. celery salt
1 T. soy sauce

Mix all ingredients. Press into 9"x13" baking dish coated with cooking spray.

Bake, covered at 375° for 20-30 minutes. Can be topped with sauce or cheese. Serves 4-6.

COLORFUL BEAN BAKE

2 c. cooked kidney beans
1 1/2 c. corn
1 1/2 c. shredded jack cheese
1 c. tomato sauce
1/2 c. chopped green chiles, drained
dash of tabasco sauce
2 c. coarsely shredded zucchini
1/4 c. corn meal
1/4 c. white bean flour
1 c. water
1 egg, beaten

In 9"x13" baking dish, combine beans, corn, tomato sauce, chiles, tabasco sauce and 1/2 of cheese; mix well. Top with zucchini.

Combine corn meal, bean flour, egg and enough water to make a pourable batter. Pour over top of veggie mixture. Bake at 350° for 20-25 minutes.

Top with remaining cheese. Bake an additional 2-3 minutes. Serves 4-6.

BURRITOS CON QUESO

1 T. olive or canola oil (opt.)
1/2 c. chopped green chiles
*2 c. refried beans or "instant mashed beans"**
* **See Cooking Options Section**

1/2 c. chopped onion
8 flour tortillas (8" size)
1/2 lb. jack cheese
1 c. salsa

Sauté onion about 2 minutes in oil or a little vegetable broth. Add chiles and beans and heat through. Spread each tortilla with bean mixture, 2 T. shredded cheese and 1-2 T. salsa. Roll and place folded side down in 9"x13" baking dish. Sprinkle with remaining cheese. Bake 15 minutes, until cheese is bubbly. Before serving, garnish with additional salsa, or Bean Gravy.

For a delicious **Bean Gravy**, to 2 c. boiling water, add 1 t. salt or seasoning substitute, 1 T. beef-flavored soup base, 1/2 t. ground cumin, 1/2 t. chili powder and 4 T. pinto bean flour. Bring to a boil and cook 2 minutes.

ORIENTAL STIR FRY

4 ribs celery
1 lg. onion
1 green pepper
2 c. 3" mung bean sprouts

1 c. sliced mushrooms
1 c. chinese cabbage
1 t. olive oil (opt.)
*1/4 t. flavored sesame oil**
3-4 T. white bean flour

*(Flavored sesame oil found in the oriental section of your supermarket is a dark oil pressed from toasted sesame seeds and is used in small quantities as a flavoring.)

Over medium-high heat, sauté veggies in olive oil or vegetable broth, adding small amounts of broth (about 2 T. at a time to create lots of steam), adding chinese cabbage last, until tender/crunchy, about 3-4 minutes. Add 2 c. boiling water, sesame oil and 2 T. chicken or vegetable base mixed with 3-4 T. white bean flour. Cook 3 minutes. Serve over hot, cooked brown rice or noodles.

LITTLE LIMA BEAN & CHILES CASSEROLES

2 c. cooked lima beans
1/2 c. chopped green onions
1/2 c. cooked chopped green chiles
2 c. cooked green beans
1 fresh or cooked tomato, diced
1 c. cheddar cheese, grated
4 eggs
2 T. white bean flour
1 t. powdered cumin
1 T. chicken or vegetable soup base

Topping:
1 c. dry bread crumbs or Okara
1 c. grated white or cottage cheese

Beat eggs, adding flour and soup base. Slightly mash lima beans. Add remaining ingredients and spoon into large muffin tins coated with cooking spray .

Bake 350° for 15-20 minutes. Mix topping ingredients and spoon on top of each little casserole and bake 5 minutes longer. Serves 6.

HOT AND SPICY BLACK BEANS AND RICE

3 c. cooked black beans
1 medium onion, chopped
1/2 c. green pepper, diced
2 T. chicken or vegetable soup base
2 c. water or bean broth
3-4 T. kidney or pinto bean flour
1/8 t. cumin
1/2 t. oregano
2 T. white vinegar
1/2 t. hot pepper sauce
1/8 t. garlic powder
1/4 c. chopped green onions
4 c. hot cooked brown rice

Combine all ingredients except green onions and rice and cook over medium heat for 10 minutes to blend flavors and thicken sauce.

Serve over hot rice and sprinkle with chopped green onions. Serves 6-8.

MUSHROOMS, BEANS AND RICE

4 c. cooked black-eyed peas
4 c. water or bean liquid
3 c. fresh, sliced mushrooms
2 c. thinly sliced celery
1 small onion, cut in strips
3 T. chicken or vegetable soup base
3/4 c. dry milk powder
1/4 c. white bean flour
4 c. cooked brown rice

Cook beans and vegetables in water over medium-high heat for 5-10 minutes, until veggies are barely tender.

Blend a small amount of cooking water with dry milk, bean flour and base. Add to bean mixture and cook 3-4 minutes more. Serve over hot brown rice.

Makes 6-8 servings

CREAMY VEGETABLE BEAN DISH

2 c. potatoes, grated
1 c. carrots, sliced
1 c. sliced cabbage or cauliflower
1 c. onions, diced or shredded
1 c. fresh or frozen corn
1 c. cooked white beans
1 c. cooked kidney beans
1 qt. boiling water
1/3 c. white bean flour
4 c. cooked brown rice

Add vegetables to boiling water and cook 15 minutes over medium heat. Mix bean flour in enough water to make a watery paste.

Stir into bean mixture and continue cooking 3 minutes, stirring occasionally. Serve over hot cooked brown rice.

Serves 6-8.

MINI CASSEROLES

1 large onion, chopped
1 green onion, chopped
1 medium carrot, grated
1 rib celery, minced
4 c. cooked white or pinto beans
2 t. chicken or vegetable soup base
2-3 tomatoes, sliced 1/4" thick
1 1/2 c. grated white cheese

In medium saucepan, cook onions, carrot and celery in 2 T. water for 4 minutes. Add beans and base and heat through.

In 6 individual custard cups, place 1/2 to 1 c. bean mixture (depending on size of cups). Top with one slice of tomato and sprinkle with 2 T. grated cheese.

Place filled cups in preheated 450° oven. Turn oven to broil and bake until cheese is brown and bubbly. Or, bake 10-15 minutes at 450°. Serves 6.

SPINACH LOAVES

1 c. cooked brown rice
1/2 c. cooked kidney beans
1/2 c. cooked brown rice or cracked wheat
2 T. chopped green onions
2 eggs
2 t. chicken or vegetable soup base
1 lb. fresh spinach, chopped
2 T. oatmeal
1 T. melted butter (opt.)
1 c. grated cheese

Mix oatmeal, butter (if used) and cheese.

Combine remaining ingredients and stir well. Fill oiled muffin tins to just below the top. Top with cheese mixture.

Bake in 350° oven for 20-25 minutes. Serves 4.

SWEET AND SOUR VEGGIES

Veggies:
2 c. cooked soybeans
1 c. 3" long mung bean sprouts
pinch garlic powder
1 onion, cut in thin strips
2 green onions, chopped
1 T. sesame seeds
1 c. unsweetened pineapple chunks, drained
1 c. ea. diagonally sliced carrots, celery, cauliflower

Cook all but soybeans and pineapple in 1/4 c. vegetable broth until crispy/tender. Add soybeans and pineapple and heat through while preparing sauce.

Sauce:
1/2 c. pineapple juice
1 t. molasses
1/4 c. honey
1 medium bell pepper
2 t. white bean flour
2 t. cornstarch
2 T. white vinegar
1/4 t. ground ginger
1 T. soy sauce

Finely chop bell pepper and simmer until tender in pineapple juice, molasses and honey. Mix remaining ingredients and add to juice mixture, stirring until thickened, about 1 minute. Makes 1 1/2 cups.

Pour thickened sauce over hot vegetable mixture. Serve over brown rice, garnished with additional sesame seeds or chopped, toasted almonds. Serves 6-8.

JAPANESE RED RICE

2 c. cooked brown rice
1 c. red bean cooking liquid or water
1 T. chicken or vegetable soup base
1 c. cooked red beans
1 chopped green onion

Using freshly cooked or frozen brown rice, combine all ingredients and bring to a boil. Cover and let rest 5 minutes. Drain off excess liquid and reserve for making soup. Serve rice plain or on a bed of steamed 3" mung bean sprouts. Serves 3-4.

TAMALE PIE

2 1/2 c. warm water
1/2 t. salt
1/2 c. pinto bean flour
1/2 c. masa or fine corn flour

In a small saucepan, bring all ingredients to a boil, then turn heat to low and cook 4 minutes. Remove from heat, add 1 c. gravy mix (below), and pour into 9"x13" pan. Let cool 5 minutes. Spread with remaining gravy. Top with ***1 c. fresh grated cheese, 1 c. fresh chopped green onions and tops.*** Serve with a *dollop of sour cream.*

Tamale Pie Gravy:
2 c. warm water
2 T. chili powder
1 1/2 T. cumin
2 T. pinto bean flour
2 T. fine corn flour or masa
1 t. chicken or vegetable bouillon

Whisk all dry ingredients into warm water. Cook 1 min on medium-high while stirring, then cover pan and turn heat to low. Cook 2 min. Add salt to taste.

SOUTHERN RED BEANS AND RICE

2 c. water or bean liquid
3 stalks celery, chopped
1/2 c. chopped mushrooms
2 T. green pepper, chopped
1 lg. yellow onion, chopped
3 c. cooked small red beans
1 -2 T. chicken or vegetable soup base
Tabasco/Picante sauce to taste
1 T. Worcestershire sauce
4 c. cooked brown rice

In saucepan, bring all ingredients except rice to a boil, then turn to low. Simmer, covered, for 15 -25 minutes. Serve over hot rice. Serves 4-6.

BEAN AND PEPPER STIR FRY

6 c. bean sprouts
3 bell peppers, cut in strips
1/2 t. sesame oil
1/8 t. garlic powder
1/2 to 1 t. ground ginger
2 T. soy sauce
4 c. cooked brown rice or linguini

In saucepan, bring peppers, bean sprouts and 2 T. water to a boil, then cover and simmer for 2-3 minutes. (Veggies should still be crisp.)

Drain off any excess liquid and add remaining ingredients. In a heavy skillet or wok, stir fry for 1 minute.

Serve over hot cooked rice or pasta. Serves 4-6.

INDONESIAN BLACK BEANS AND FRIED RICE

1 c. cooked black beans
2 t. canola oil or 4 T. vegetable broth
2 eggs, beaten
1 finely chopped small onion
1 c. finely diced cucumber
3 T. Pace's Picante Sauce
1 T. soy sauce
2 c. cooked brown rice

Heat black beans separately. Put 1 t. of the oil or 2 T. broth in a large skillet, heat, and add eggs, tipping to spread to edges of pan.

Cook over medium heat until top surface dulls. Cut into thin strips, remove from pan and set aside.

Add remaining oil or broth to pan and stir fry onion and cucumber for 1 minute. Add rice and sauces and stir-fry 1 1/2 minutes, or until heated through.

Place on serving dish and garnish with black beans and egg strips. Serves 4.

RED AND YELLOW DINNER

2 c. cooked kidney beans
2 T. olive or canola oil (opt.)
3 T. Pace's Picante Sauce
2 T. chicken or vegetable soup base
1 t. ground turmeric
1/2 t. ground cumin
1/2 t. ground coriander
2 c. hot cooked brown rice

Heat kidney beans separately.

Add remaining ingredients to a large skillet and stir-fry or simmer until heated through. Place rice on a serving dish and mound hot kidney beans in the center.

Serve with green salad. Serves 4.

Note: ***The following recipes have been made with soybeans in one form or another, but ANY bean may be substituted. Each bean has a slightly different taste, so the recipe will taste a little different with each bean.***

SPANISH RICE AND BEANS

2 T. canola oil or 1/4 c. water
2 c. cooked rice
1 c. cooked chopped soybeans
2 c. fresh diced tomatoes
3 T. chopped green peppers
1 onion, chopped
1 t. salt
1/4 t. pepper
1 T. chicken or vegetable soup base
1 t. cumin

Stir-fry all ingredients in heavy skillet until heated through and vegetables are crunchy-tender.

Serves 4. Top with grated cheese, if desired.

SUKIYAKI SUPREME

1 c. thinly sliced onions
1 c. thinly sliced celery
1 c. sliced mushrooms
1/2 c. sliced green peppers
1 c. cooked soybeans
1/2 c. thinly sliced carrots
1/2 c. chopped green onions

Sauce:
1 c. soy sauce
1 t. chicken or vegetable soup base
1/4 t. pepper
3/4 c. water
2 T. honey
1/2 t. molasses

Simmer or steam vegetables in 1/4 c. water for 3-5 minutes, until tender/ crunchy.

Add sauce ingredients and thicken, if desired, with 3-4 T. cornstarch. Serve over pasta or brown rice.

Serves 4-6.

CHILI-NOODLE DISH

4 c. cooked soybeans
1 medium onion, chopped
1 bell pepper, chopped
2 c. tomato sauce
4 c. cooked noodles
1 c. celery, chopped
1 1/2 c. corn
1 4 1/2 oz. can chopped olives
1 T. chili powder
1 1/2 t. garlic powder

Chop or grind beans to hamburger-like consistency. Heat tomato sauce, celery, onion and pepper over medium heat 5 minutes.

Add remaining ingredients except noodles and heat through. Add noodles and put mixture into a 9"x13" baking dish coated with cooking spray.

Cover and bake 20 minutes at 350°. May be topped with 2 c. grated cheese, if desired. Serves 6.

SIDE DISHES

With the addition of beans to these recipes, Side Dishes provide good quality protein to complement any meal... Or, they can be served as a meal by themselves.

The FAST Refried Beans in this section can be also be served as a dip, or as a burrito, enchilada or sandwich filling.

All recipes in this section are Gluten-Free.

MEXICAN PILAF

1 1/2 c. cooked brown rice
*1 c. cooked cracked beans**
2 eggs, beaten
1 c. sliced mushrooms
1/2 c. chopped green onions
1/2 c. finely shredded carrots
1-2 T. canola oil (opt.)
1/2 c. hot water
1/4 t. each chili powder, cumin
1/2 t. chicken or vegetable soup base

*See Cooking Options Section.

Combine rice, beans and eggs; mix thoroughly. In medium skillet, sauté vegetables until tender. Add rice mixture.

Cook, stirring, for 3-4 minutes, until mixture is fluffy and lightly browned. Add combined water and flavorings; continue cooking 3-5 minutes or until liquid is absorbed, stirring occasionally.

Serves 4-6.

ORIENTAL PILAF

1 1/2 c. cooked brown rice
*1 c. cooked cracked beans**
2 eggs, beaten
1 c. sliced mushrooms
1/2 c. chopped green onions
1/2 c. finely chopped celery
1 c. frozen petite peas
*1/4 t. sesame oil**
1 1/2 T. canola oil (opt.)
2 T. soy sauce
2 t. honey
1/2 t. chicken or vegetable soup base
1/2 t. ginger
1/2 c. hot water

*See Cooking Options Section.

Combine rice, beans and eggs; mix thoroughly. In large skillet, sauté vegetables (except peas) in oil or water until tender. Add rice mixture.

Cook, stirring, for 3-4 minutes, until mixture is fluffy and lightly browned. Add combined water, soy sauce, honey, chicken flavoring and ginger; continue cooking 3-5 minutes or until liquid is absorbed, stirring occasionally. Add peas; heat through. Serves 4-6.

GREEN RICE PILAF

2 c. cooked brown rice
1/2 c. cooked lentils
2 T. canola oil or 4 T. water
1 T. finely chopped parsley
1 large onion, finely diced
1/2 c. chopped green pepper
1/2 c. finely sliced celery
1/3 c. sliced fresh mushrooms
1/2 c. chopped almonds
1 c. hot water
1 T. chicken or vegetable soup base

Sauté fresh veggies in oil or water in large skillet. Add remaining ingredients; cover and simmer for about 15 minutes, or until liquid is absorbed and mixture is dry and fluffy. Serves 4-6.

MEXICAN FIESTA BLEND VEGETABLES

1/2 c. ea. cooked white, garbanzo and kidney beans
2 c. broccoli pieces
1 c. green beans
1 c. whole kernel corn
1 c. thinly sliced carrots
1 T. chopped pimientos (opt.)
1 T. Picante sauce
1/2 t. chicken or vegetable soup base
1/4 t. chili powder

In medium saucepan over medium-high heat, bring vegetables and 3 T. water to a boil. Cover with a tight-fitting lid and turn heat to low. Simmer for 5-8 minutes. Add seasonings. Serves 4-6.

ORIENTAL BLEND VEGETABLES

2 c. french sliced green beans
3/4 c. diagonally sliced carrots
3/4 c. cooked red beans
3/4 c. shredded Napa cabbage
1/2 c. sliced water chestnuts
1/2 c. sliced cauliflower
2 t. sesame seeds
1 t. soy sauce

In medium saucepan over medium-high heat, bring vegetables and 3 T. water to a boil. Cover with a tight-fitting lid and turn heat to low. Simmer for 5-8 minutes. Serves 4-6.

ORIENTAL OMELETTES

4 eggs
1/2 t. sesame oil
1 T. chopped fresh parsley

Filling:
2 green onions, chopped
1 c. very finely sliced celery
1 c. 3-day mung bean sprouts
2 T. soy sauce
pinch of ground ginger

Beat eggs. Mix filling ingredients. Coat hot, heavy skillet with cooking spray. Put 2 T. of the beaten egg and spread it out to make a tiny omelette.

When the underside has set, put a small portion of the filling mixture on one side of the omelette. Fold over the other side and transfer the omelette to a plate. Cover to keep warm.

Repeat with remaining ingredients. Return cooked omelettes in skillet, cover, and cook over low heat to heat through. Serve topped with sauce and garnished with parsley.

Sauce:
2 T. cornstarch
1/2 c. hot water
1/2 t. chicken or vegetable soup base
1 T. soy sauce
1 T. barbecue sauce or catsup

Mix cornstarch into soy sauce and catsup.

Add all ingredients to hot water and cook in a small saucepan over medium-high heat for 2-3 minutes, or just until thick.

Sauce may be made in large batches, refrigerated, and used as a gravy for patties, loaves, omelettes.

REFRIED BEANS READY IN ONLY 5 MINUTES!

2 1/4 c. warm water
1/2 to 3/4 t. salt
tiny pinch garlic powder (opt.)
3/4 c. pinto or black bean flour
1/4 t. cumin
1/2 t. chili powder

In a small saucepan, whisk dry ingredients into water. Bring water to a boil.

Cook, while stirring, over medium heat for 1 minute, until mixture thickens. Don't worry about lumps - they taste great too!

Reduce heat to low, cover pan and cook 4 minutes. Add 1/2 c. Picante sauce, if desired. (Mixture thickens as it cools and will stay thick even after heating.)

"INSTANT" REFRIED BEAN MIX

1 1/2 c. pinto or black bean flour
1 1/2 t. chili powder
1/8 t. garlic powder (opt.)
1/2 t. cumin
1 1/2 t. salt
1 t. instant minced onions (opt.)

Mix and store in airtight container.

To prepare, whisk 3/4 c. above mixture into 2 1/4 c. warm water in a small saucepan. Cook as above, adding your favorite salsa after cooking.

Note: When using **black beans**, the cooked mixture will be a blue-gray-brown color because of the very short cooking time. This isn't objectionable when using this recipe for burrito filling, but if you want to serve it as a dip, microwave cooked mixture in a covered dish for about 5 minutes on high. This helps achieve a better brown color.

I like to make up a triple batch of this mixture and keep it in the refrigerator. I can always have an almost "instant" meal ready within a few minutes.

This makes a great present for a **"Gift of a Healthy Heart."** Package in a calico bag or decorated glass jar. Include a recipe for Refried Beans (above).

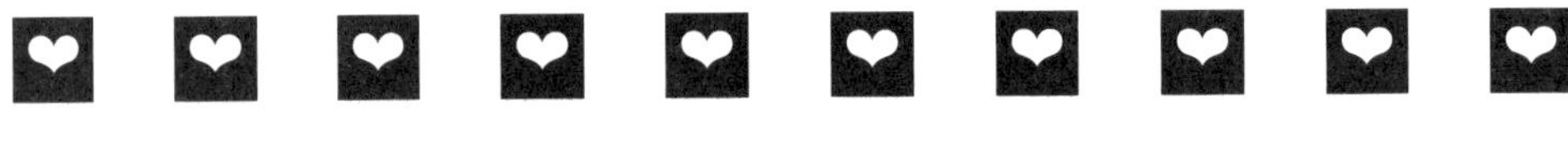

COMPANY DINNERS

*Your company will **love** the Quiche, Crepes, Individual "meat"loaves, and Stir-fry in this section... and they will never know you've added BEANS to these scrumptious recipes!*

Most recipes in this section are Gluten-Free or can be made with Gluten-Free breads.

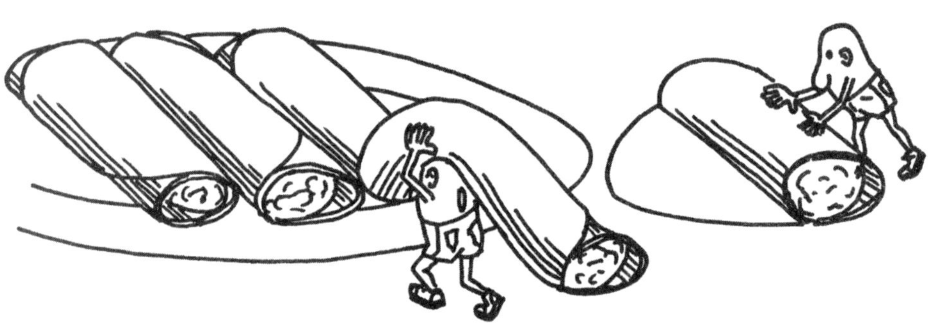

QUICHE - VERSATILE, QUICK AND CLASSY

An easy rule of thumb guide for making up your own recipes is to start with *1 egg, 1 c. water, 1 c. tofu, 2 T. bean flour, 2 T. dry milk powder, 1/2 t. salt, dash white pepper and 1 c. shredded cheese* (variety depends on taste desired in recipe).

Add *2 c. cooked or frozen vegetable*s and season to taste with herbs or commercial seasoning mixes.

NOTE: To cook faster, place pastry in smaller containers and bake until center is almost set, OR omit pastry and bake in muffin tins coated with cooking spray.

VEGETABLE BEAN QUICHE

Basic Sauce:

1 egg
2 T. white bean flour
1 c. tofu
1 c. water
3 T dry milk powder
dash white pepper
1/2 t. salt (opt.)
1 c. shredded cheese (opt.)

•••

2 t. Country Blend All Purpose Seasoning (see p. 65)
1/2 c. chopped mushrooms
1/2 c. cooked white or pink beans
1/4 c. chopped green onions
2 T. butter or olive oil (opt.)
3/4 c. fresh or frozen broccoli pieces or mixed vegetables

Blend sauce ingredients (except cheese) 2 minutes, until very smooth. Bake pricked 9" pastry shell at 375° for 5 minutes.

Pour sauce into shell. Add remaining ingredients. Bake in a 325° oven for 50 minutes or until the center is nearly set.

(See next page for Variations)

QUICHE VARIATIONS:

CHICKEN AND BROCCOLI QUICHE

Mix Basic Sauce. Add the following:

1 T. chicken or vegetable soup base
1 1/2 c. cooked broccoli tops
1/4 c. finely chopped onion
1/2 c. sliced mushrooms

Follow instructions on p. 125.

ZUCCHINI QUICHE

Mix Basic Sauce. Add the following:

1 1/2 c. coarsely shredded zucchini, mixed with 1/2 t. salt and allowed to drain 10 minutes.
1/2 c. thinly sliced cauliflower
1/4 c. chopped red bell pepper
1 T. chicken or vegetable soup base

Follow instructions on p. 125.

MEXICAN BEAN QUICHE

Mix Basic Sauce. Add the following:

1 c. cooked pinto or kidney beans
1/4 c. chopped green pepper
3/4 c. whole kernel corn
2 T. mild Picante Sauce
1/2 t. cumin
1/4 t. salt (opt.)
1/4 c. finely chopped onions

Follow instructions on p. 125.

ORIENTAL BEANS AND RICE QUICHE

Mix Basic Sauce. Add the following:

1 T. soy sauce
1/2 c. chopped water chestnuts
2 T. sesame seeds
*1/8 t. sesame oil (toasted)**
1/4 c. chopped green onions
1 c. raw 3" mung bean sprouts
1/4 c. cooked brown rice
1 c. oriental noodles for topping

*See Cooking Options

Follow instructions on p. 125. Top with oriental noodles before baking.

ORIENTAL SPINACH QUICHE

Mix Basic Sauce. Add the following:

1 c. mushrooms, sliced
*1/8 t. sesame oil (toasted)**
1/4-1/2 t. salt
2 T. chopped green onions
2 c. frozen spinach, drained

*See Cooking Options

Follow instructions on p. 125.

LINGUINE WITH CRAB SAUCE

1 lb. linguine or spaghetti
3 c. hot water
1 T. crab soup base
1/2 t. Fines Herbs
6 T. white bean flour
2 T. chopped parsley for garnish
salt to taste

Cook linguini according to package directions. Drain. In saucepan, over medium heat, mix remaining ingredients with wire whip. Cook until thickened, then reduce heat and simmer 3 minutes. Serve hot over cooked noodles.

CHEESEY BEANS IN CREPES

12 to 14 crepes

Filling:

1 10 oz. package frozen chopped spinach or 3/4 pound fresh spinach
3 c. cooked lima beans, mashed
2 t. chicken or vegetable soup base
1/2 c. sliced onions
2 c. sliced mushrooms
2 T. minced green onion
1 T. olive or canola oil (opt.)

In medium saucepan, cook spinach in 1 T. water, then remove from pan and drain.

In same pan, sauté mushrooms and onions in oil or vegetable broth, then add remaining filling ingredients and heat through, adding 1-2 T. spinach cooking water if necessary.

Cheese sauce:

2 T. butter (opt.)
4 T. wheat flour
1 T. garbanzo or navy bean flour
3 c. warm water
1 t. chicken or vegetable soup base
dash white pepper
2 eggs
1 c. grated low-fat cheese

Blend sauce ingredients except cheese and pour into a saucepan. Cook over medium heat until thickened. Stir in cheese until it melts. Remove from heat.

Spread 1/3 c. filling mixture in the center of each crepe. Roll and place seam side down in a baking dish coated with cooking spray.

Fill with remaining crepes, placing them close together. Top with enough sauce to cover.

If desired, add an additional 1 c. grated low-fat cheese or fat-free cottage cheese on top. Cover with foil. Bake at 400° for 20 minutes. Serve with remaining sauce. Serves 6-8.

CREPES WITH HOT "CRAB" FILLING

6-8 crepes
1 1/2 c. real crab or simmered "crab" pieces (see Meals In Minutes, cheese section)
1/2 c. tofu, cut in 1/4" squares
2 c. chopped celery
1 T. finely chopped onion
1 t. dried parsley flakes
1/8 t. dried basil leaves
1 c. fat-free mayonnaise
1 T. lemon juice
1/2 t. salt

Sauté celery and onion in skillet coated with cooking spray for 1 minute. Add remaining ingredients and heat through.

Place 1/2 c. mixture in each crepe. Roll up and place in serving dish.

If desired, top with grated mozzarella cheese; place in oven and bake at 400° until cheese melts. OR, serve topped with White Bean Gravy (p. 61)

MEXICAN MINI LOAVES

1 c. mild taco sauce
1/2 c. cooked mushroom pieces
2 T. chopped green onion
1 egg
1-2 c. grated cheese or cottage cheese
3/4 c. oatmeal
*1/3 c. mashed pinto beans**
4 T. chopped ripe olives
1 c. cooked brown rice
1 t. chicken or vegetable soup base
1/2 t. each chili powder, cumin, oregano basil

*See Cooking Options for "Instant Mashed Beans"

Mix all ingredients, saving out 1/2 c. cheese and 2 T. olives.

Shape into 3 to 6 mini-loaves on a baking sheet coated with cooking spray. OR, press into 9"x13" baking pan coated with cooking spray.

Bake at 375° for 15-20 minutes. Top with remaining cheese and olives and return to oven to melt.

ITALIAN MINI–TOFU LOAVES

3/4 c. oatmeal
2 t. chicken or vegetable soup base
1/8 t. garlic powder
1 egg
1 T. finely diced onion
1 T. white bean flour
2 t. Italian dressing
1 c. cooked brown rice
1 c. mashed Tofu
1 c. grated mozzarella cheese
1 c. tomato sauce
1 4 1/2 oz. can chopped ripe olives

Combine all ingredients, reserving 1/2 of cheese, tomato sauce and olives. Mix thoroughly. Shape into small loaves or fill muffin tins nearly full.

Cover with foil and bake at 375° 20-30 minutes, or until set. Top with remaining sauce, cheese, then olives. Bake 5 more minutes. Serves 4-6.

ASPARAGUS–TOMATO STIR FRY

1 lb. fresh asparagus or broccoli stems
4 green onions, diagonally sliced
1 1/2 c. sliced fresh mushrooms
1 c. cubed firm tofu
2 t. canola oil or 1/4 c. water
8-10 drops flavored sesame oil (opt.)
2 t. soy sauce
1 t. sesame seeds
1/4 t. salt (opt.)
1 T. warm water
2 t. white bean flour
2 small tomatoes, diced
•••
Hot cooked brown rice

Cut tender portions of asparagus and bias-slice into 1 1/2" lengths. (Or peel broccoli stems and cut diagonally into 1/4" slices.)

In a preheated wok or large, heavy skillet, add 1 t. oil or 2 T. water and heat 30 seconds over medium-high or high heat. Stir fry tougher peeled asparagus or broccoli stems 1 minute, then add tender tops and green onions. Cook until crunchy/tender. Set aside.

Cook tofu and mushrooms in 1 t. oil or 2 T. water for 30 seconds. While stirring, sprinkle cooked vegetables with bean flour to coat, then add the 1 T warm water, soy sauce, sesame seeds and salt. Cook and stir 1 minute. Add cooked asparagus and onions, diced tomatoes, and heat through. Serve over cooked rice.

SNACKS

The nutritious recipes in this section are high in both protein and carbohydrates to give you a real energy boost — with a NO-fat snack!

With little or no supervision, these recipes can be made by children of all ages. "Squirt Bottle" corn or wheat chips are fun to make and a real treat to eat. See how creative your children can be with these recipes.

With only "good-for-you" calories in these snacks, you can eat a "bunch!"

Most recipes in this section are Gluten-Free.

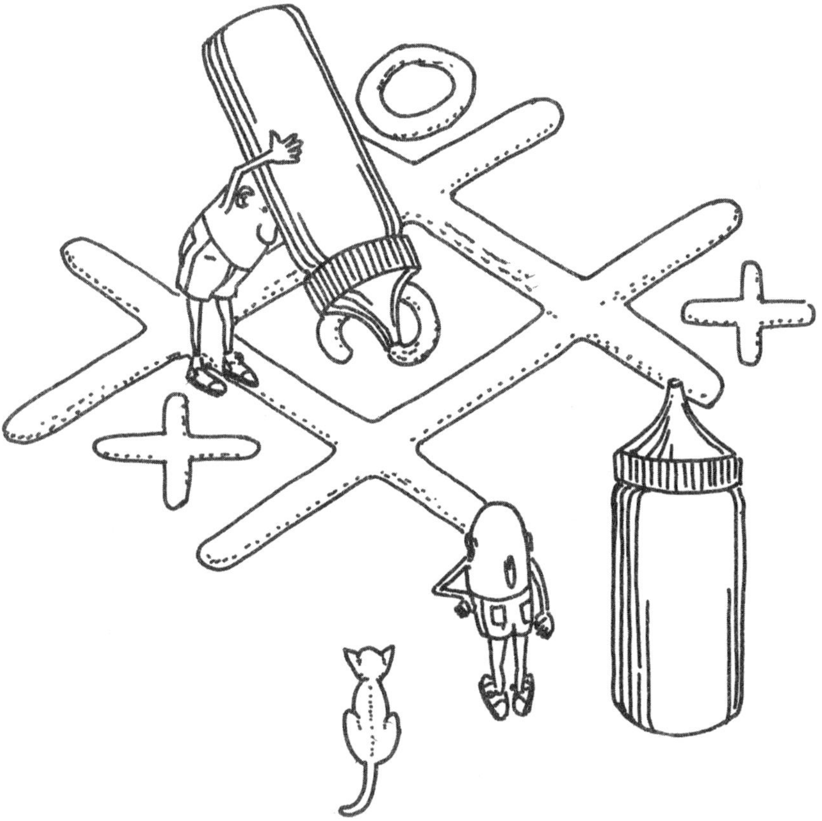

SUPER CORN CHIPS (Wheat-Free)

1/2 c. fine corn flour
1 t. fine pea flour
1/2 c. water
1/2 t. Country Blend All Purpose Seasoning (see p. 65)
1/8 t. garlic powder
1/4 t. onion powder
1/8 to 1/4 t. salt

Blend just until smooth. Spoon batter, 1 t. at a time, into circles on a baking sheet lightly coated with cooking spray. (If too much spray is used, chips will not get crisp, so lightly spray, then, if necessary, wipe tray with a paper towel to remove excess.)

Tilt to spread very thin, turning pan as you tilt to maintain circle shape. Bake at 350° for 8 minutes, or until edges curl and center is set. Turn over; bake another 2-5 minutes until golden and crisp.

Note: Thinner crackers cook faster, so if your chips are not crisp following above instructions, spread thinner or add a little more water to batter. (Mixture thickens after standing for 15 minutes or more, so you may want to add more water to thin.)

For **Squirt Bottle Crackers**, place batter in an empty honey bear with small nozzle opening. Squirt and spread dough in circles with the nozzle. Follow instructions above.

GREAT WHEAT CHIPS (Salt-Free)

1 c. + 2 T. water
1 t. white bean flour
1/2 c. whole wheat flour
1/2 t. any no-salt seasoning blend

Blend water and flours until smooth. Stir in seasoning. Spoon batter onto a baking sheet lightly coated with cooking spray. Sprinkle each circle of batter lightly with sesame seeds, poppy seeds or Parmesan Cheese.

Bake as above.

Try a variety of seasonings in the chip batter. Although many of the packaged powdered seasoning mixes do contain salt, they make an excellent less salty chip than potato chips, and without frying! Use 1/2 t. to 1 1/2 t. packaged mix, depending on the brand.

REFRIED BEANS - See Side Dishes Section, p. 123.

Fast Refried Beans can be made in only 5 minutes, then served as a chip dip, enchilada or burrito filling, or spread on Mexican Pizza, then topped with salsa and toppings of your choice.

ZIPPY BEAN DIP

2 c. cooked pinto beans
2 T. fat-free mayonnaise
1 t. Worcestershire sauce
2 T. lemon juice
1 T. chopped green chiles
1/4 c. chopped green onions
salt to taste

Mash beans. Mix with remaining ingredients, reserving 2 T. of onions for garnish. Serve with crisp raw veggies or corn chips.

TACO FLAVORED SNAX

*1/2 c. moist Okara**
1-2 T. dry Taco Seasoning Mix

*See the section on Tofu and Okara to make this versatile snack food from soybeans.

Mix thoroughly; spread on baking sheet coated with cooking spray and bake at 300° for 10-15 minutes, until dry and crunchy. Store in an air-tight container.

Drying options: This can be dried in an oven, dehydrator, in the sun or near a wood stove or a heater.

VARIATIONS TO TACO FLAVORED SNAX -

to 1/2 c. moist Okara, add one of the following seasonings, then dry as above:

Apple-Cinnamon Snax - Add 1/2 c. dried apple dices, 1/2 t. vanilla, 1 T. brown sugar and 1/4 t. cinnamon

Sesame-Ginger Snax - Add 1/2 t. chicken or vegetable soup base, 1/4 t. ginger, 1 t. soy sauce and 1 T. sesame seeds

FOR CASSEROLE TOPPINGS OR AS A BREADING, add spice mixes to taste, dry in oven, and store in glass jars until ready to use.

COOKIES AND BARS

Desserts containing wheat flour provide an exceptionally easy way to incorporate bean flours by simply replacing up to 1/4 wheat flour with bean flour. If a recipe calls for 1 c. wheat flour, I use 3/4 c. wheat flour and 1/4 c. white bean flour, which is the lightest in color and has the most bland flavor.

To begin substituting this flour in your recipes, start with 2 T. bean flour per cup of wheat flour, and gradually work up to 1/4 the total amount of wheat flour.

The Gluten-Free flour mix on page 6 can be used in place of wheat flour.

RASPBERRY OAT BARS

1 3/4 c. rolled oats
1 1/4 c. whole wheat flour
1/4 c. white bean flour
3/4 c. honey
1/2 c. chopped nuts
1/2 t. baking soda
3/4 c. melted butter or applesauce
2 c. fresh or frozen raspberries
1/2 c. honey
3 T. water
2 T. cornstarch
2 t. lemon juice

Heat oven to 350°. Combine oats, flours, nuts, baking soda and salt. Add butter or applesauce and 3/4 c. honey, mixing until crumbly.

Reserve 3/4 c. mixture; press remaining mixture onto bottom of 9"x13" baking dish coated with cooking spray. Bake 8 minutes.

Meanwhile, combine berries, remaining honey and 2 T. of the water. Bring to a boil; simmer 2 minutes. Mix cornstarch, remaining water and lemon juice and gradually stir into berry mixture; cook and stir about 30 seconds or until thickened.

Spread over partially baked mixture; sprinkle with reserved oat mixture. Bake 15-18 minutes or until topping is golden brown. Cool; cut into bars.

NO-WHEAT DATE COOKIES

1/2 c. peanut or almond butter
2 eggs
1 T. vanilla
3 T. garbanzo bean flour
1/4 t. salt (opt.)
1 t. baking powder
1 c. ea. chopped dates, raisins nuts, shredded coconut

Beat nut butter, eggs and vanilla until smooth and fluffy. Mix in remaining ingredients. Form into 1 1/2" thick rolls.

Slice 1/4" thick. Bake at 350° for 8-10 minutes, or until browned on the bottom.

BANANA ORANGE BARS

3 large bananas, mashed
1/4 c. oil or applesauce
1/2 c. orange juice
2 eggs
2 t. vanilla
1/2 c. melted honey
2 c. rolled oats
1 t. grated orange peel
1/4 c. pea or white bean flour
2 c. whole wheat or GF flour
3/4 t. baking soda
1/2 t. salt (optional)
1/2 t. nutmeg
3/4 c. finely chopped dates
1/2 c. finely chopped nuts

Combine moist ingredients. Add remaining ingredients, mixing only until dry ingredients are moistened. Spread into 9"x13" baking dish coated with cooking spray. Bake 20-25 minutes at 350° or until light golden brown. Cut into bars.

These can be sprinkled with powdered Sucanat* or served with orange-flavored honey butter.

Orange-flavored Honey Butter

1/2 c. softened butter
1 t. grated orange peel
1/3 c. soft honey
1/2 t. vanilla
few drops orange extract (opt.)

In mixing bowl, combine all ingredients and beat at high speed with electric mixer until light and fluffy. Refrigerate. Great as a frosting, cookie or cracker filling, or on bread.

SPICY APPLESAUCE COOKIES

1/2 c. oil or applesauce
1 c. honey
1 c. applesauce
1 t. vanilla
1 t. baking soda
1 t. baking powder
1/2 t. salt
1 1/2 t. cinnamon
1/4 t. allspice
1 c. raisins
2/3 c. chopped almonds
2 1/2 c. Rita's GF flour

Beat all but flour. Stir in flour until moistened. Spoon onto baking sheet coated with non-stick vegetable spray. Bake at 350 for 12-15 minutes. Makes 2 dozen.

HONEY BANANA COOKIES

1/2 c. chunky peanut butter
1/4 c. canola oil or applesauce
1 c. honey
1 medium banana, mashed
1 t. vanilla
1 egg
1 c. buttermilk
1 t. soda
1 t. baking powder
1/4 t. salt
1/2 t. cinnamon
1/4 t. nutmeg
2 1/2 c. Rita's GF flour
1/2 c. ea. chopped nuts and carob chips

Combine all but flour , nuts and chips and beat well. Add remaining ingredients and stir until moistened. Spoon onto baking tray coated with cooking spray and bake at 350° for 15 minutes. Makes 3 dozen.

CAROB FRUIT SQUARES

1 c. 3-day sprouted wheat
1 c. pitted dates
3/4 c. toasted coconut
*1/4 c. dry Okara**
*See Tofu and Okara Section.
1/2 c. melted carob chips
1/2 c. chunky peanut butter
1 t. vanilla

Grind wheat and dates in a hand grinder. In a microwave or double boiler, heat peanut butter, vanilla and carob chips to melt. Reserving 1/2 coconut and Okara, combine all ingredients; mix well. Press into 8" square pan and top with reserved coconut mixture. Cool and cut into 1" squares.

This is also excellent with 1/4 c. yogurt cream cheese (see *Natural* Meals In Minutes, cheeses section) added to peanut butter mixture.

APPLE-BEAN COOKIES

1/2 c. canola oil or applesauce
1 c. honey
*1 c. mashed white beans**
1/2 c. applesauce
2 t. soda
2 1/2 c. whole wheat or GF flour
1 egg
1/2 t. cinnamon
1/2 t. cloves
1/2 t. nutmeg
1/2 t. salt
1 c. raisins
1 c. nuts, chopped
1 c. rolled oats

Cream oil or applesauce, honey, mashed beans (See Cooking Options Section for "Instant Mashed Beans.") and applesauce. Add remaining ingredients. Chill dough one hour. Drop by teaspoon on baking sheet coated with cooking spray; bake at 375° for 10 minutes.

CAROB AND SOY BROWNIES

1/2 c. butter or applesauce
2/3 c. honey
2 eggs
1 t. vanilla
1/2 t. salt
1 t. dry milk powder
1/2 c. carob powder
1/2 c. whole wheat or GF flour
1/3 c. soy flour
1 t. baking powder
1 c. chopped nuts
1 c. warm water

Cream butter or applesauce and honey; add eggs one at a time, then vanilla, beating well after each addition. Add combined dry ingredients, stirring just until moistened.

Bake in 9" square pan coated with cooking spray at 350° for 30 minutes. Hot brownies can be topped with 1 c. carob chips, spreading evenly to frost as chips melt.

Note: Wheat germ or bran may be substituted for soy flour.

MILLION $$ BARS (SUPER RICH!)

1 3/4 c. whole wheat or GF flour
1/4 c. white bean flour
1 c. oil or applesauce
1 1/2 c. honey
1 c. cooked prunes, chopped
1 c. chopped nuts
1 c. buttermilk
1 1/2 c. raisins
3 eggs, beaten
1 t. soda
1 t. cinnamon
1 t. nutmeg
1 t. salt
2 t. vanilla

Mix all ingredients and pour into 11" x 15" or larger pan that has been sprayed with a non-stick coating.

Bake at 350° for 25 minutes, or until toothpick inserted in center of batter comes out clean. Cut into squares, dust with powdered sugar, if desired, and serve hot or cold.

(The larger the pan, the thinner the bars and the shorter the baking time.)

SPICY APPLE COOKIES

1 1/2 c. whole wheat flour
1/4 c. white bean flour
1 c. quick oatmeal
1/2 t. baking powder
1/2 t. baking soda
1/4 t. salt
1/2 t. ground cinnamon
1/4. t. ground cloves
1/2 c. canola oil or applesauce
3/4 c. honey
1 t. vanilla
1/2 t. lemon juice
2 eggs
1 1/2 c. grated apples
*1/4 c. mashed beans**
1 c. raisins
1 c. chopped dates
1 c. chopped walnuts

*See Cooking Options Section for "Instant Mashed Beans."

Mix dry ingredients. Cream oil or applesauce, honey, vanilla, lemon juice and eggs. Add remaining ingredients and mix well.

Drop by teaspoons onto baking sheets that have been sprayed with a non-stick coating. Bake at 358° for 12-15 minutes, or until lightly browned. 3-4 dozen cookies.

RICH OATMEAL BUTTERSCOTCH CHIP COOKIES

1 c. butter, softened, or applesauce
3/4 c. firmly packed brown sugar
1/2 c. honey
1 egg
1 t. vanilla
2 T. white bean flour
1 t. baking soda
1 t. salt
3 c. quick oats
2 c. butterscotch chips
1 1/2 c. whole wheat flour
1 1/2 c. chopped nuts

Beat together butter, sugar and honey until fluffy. Beat in egg and vanilla. Add dry ingredients and mix well.

Drop by rounded teaspoonfuls onto ungreased cookie sheet. Bake at 350° for 9 to 11 minutes.

PEANUT BUTTER BANANA BARS

2 eggs, beaten
1/3 c. peanut butter
1/4 c. honey
2 T. garbanzo bean flour
1/2 c. whole wheat or GF flour
1/2 c. chopped nuts
1/4 c. coconut
1/2 t. ground cinnamon
1/4 t. salt
1 large ripe banana, chopped

Combine all ingredients and mix well.

Pour into an 8" square baking pan that has been sprayed with a non-stick coating and bake at 350° for 15 minutes. Cut into bars while still warm.

HONEY RAISIN COOKIES

1 c. water
2 c. raisins or dates
1/2 c. canola oil or applesauce
1 1/2 c. honey
3 eggs
1 t. vanilla
3 1/2 c. whole wheat or GF flour
1/2 c. white bean flour
1 t. baking powder
1 t. baking soda
1 t. ground cinnamon
1/4 t. ea. nutmeg and allspice
1/2 t. salt
1 c. chopped nuts
1 c. wheat germ or okara

Boil water and raisins in a saucepan 5 minutes. Cool.

Beat oil or applesauce, honey, eggs and vanilla. Add cooled raisin mixture and remaining ingredients, including enough wheat germ or okara to make a stiff batter that can be dropped by teaspoons on a baking sheet that has been sprayed with a non-stick coating.

Bake for 12-15 minutes, or until lightly browned. Cook on a wire rack.

PEANUT BUTTER MOUNDS

1 c. chunky peanut butter
1/4 c. butter (opt.)
3/4 c. honey
1 1/4 c. whole wheat flour
1/4 c. white bean flour
1 t. baking powder
1/2 c. oatmeal
1 egg
1/2 c. peanuts
1 c. carob or butterscotch chips

Combine in order given and drop by spoonfuls onto baking sheet that has been sprayed with a non-stick coating.

Bake 8-12 minutes at 350°. Makes 3-4 dozen.

HONEY GRAHAM CRACKERS

1 3/4 c. whole wheat flour
1/4 c. white bean flour
1/3 c. dry milk powder
1/4 t. soda
scant t. baking powder
1/2 t. cinnamon
pinch of salt

Mix in a bowl. Make a nest and add:

1/3 c. oil
1/2 c. soft honey
1 t. vinegar or lemon juice
1 T. vanilla
2 T. water

Mix until well moistened. As wheat flours differ in moisture content, you may need to add more or less wheat flour to stiffen or soften dough.

Roll out 1/8" thick on baking sheet (one without sides works best) that has been sprayed with a non-stick coating. Score into small or large squares, or cut shapes with cookie cutters.

For large shapes, prick with a fork. Bake at 350° 8-10 minutes, or until golden brown. Makes 1 lg. tray.

CAROB CHIP MINT COOKIES

1/4 c. canola oil or applesauce
2 eggs
2/3 c. honey
1 1/2 c. whole wheat or GF flour
1 T. baking powder
1/4 t. salt (opt.)
2 T. white bean flour
1 T. carob powder
1/2 t. mint flavoring
1 c. walnuts
1 c. carob chips

Whip eggs,oil or applesauce and honey to creamy texture. Add remaining ingredients and mix well. Dough should be stiff. Drop by teaspoonful onto baking sheet coated with non-stick vegetable spray. Bake at 350° for 8-10 minutes. If cookies spread out too far while baking, refrigerate dough 1/2 hour, then bake as directed.

RIBBON COOKIES

1/2 c. canola oil or applesauce
2/3 c. honey
2 t. vanilla
2 eggs
1/2 t. ginger
1/4 t. salt (opt.)
1 1/2 c. whole wheat or GF flour
1/2 c. white bean flour
1 1/3 c. ribbon coconut
1 c. chopped dates or raisins

Beat oil or applesauce, honey, vanilla and eggs. Add remaining ingredients, beating lightly after each addition. Drop by teaspoonful onto baking sheet coated with non-stick vegetable spray. Bake at 350° for 8-10 minutes. If cookies spread out too far while baking, refrigerate dough 1/2 hour, then bake as directed.

GINGERBREAD BARS

1/2 c. honey
1/4 c. canola oil or applesauce
2 eggs
1/4 c. light molasses
1/2 c. buttermilk
1/8 c. white bean flour
1 1/2 c. Gluten-Free flour
1 t. ginger
1 t. cinnamon
1/2 t. ea. baking soda and baking powder
1/2 c. raisins
1/2 c. almonds, coarsely chopped

Beat honey, oil or applesauce, eggs and molasses until creamy. Add remaining ingredients and mix until just moistened. Pour into a 9"x13" baking dish that has been sprayed with a non-stick coating. Bake 20 to 25 minutes at 350°. Cut into 3" squares and sprinkle with powdered sugar.

PUDDINGS, PIES AND CAKES

Beans in Puddings, Pies and Cakes??? Desserts are often the best way to introduce beans, because no one will ever suspect!

Bean flour can be added in small quantities to any baked goods without a change in flavor or texture. This addition also makes your dessert a complete protein, so you can serve these nutritious deserts more often!

The Gluten-Free flour mix on page 6 can be used in place of wheat flour in nearly all the recipes in this section.

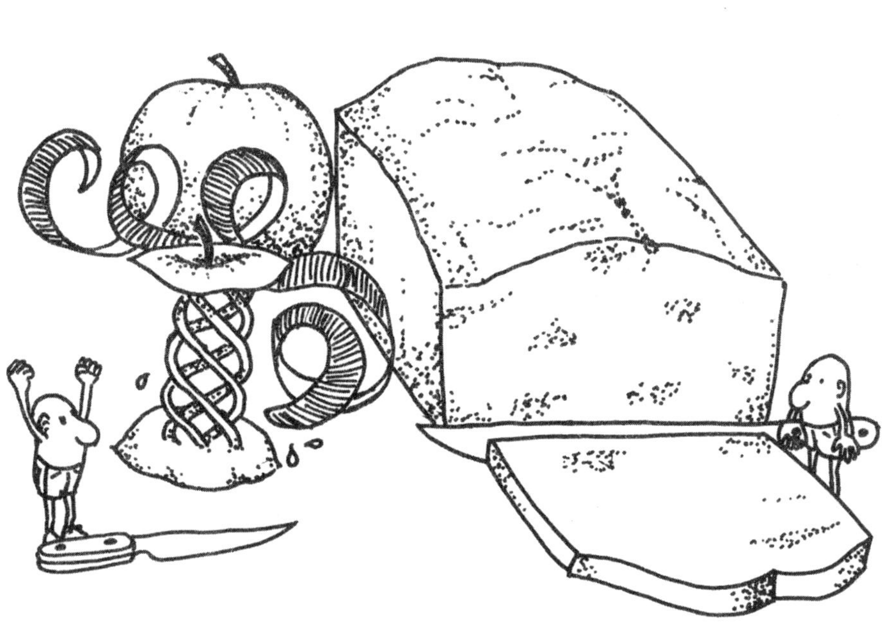

GRANDMA'S BEST DATE NUT PUDDING

1 c. dates
1 t. soda
1 c. boiling water
2 T. canola oil or applesauce
1 c. honey
2 c. whole wheat or GF flour
1/2 c. white bean flour
1 t. baking powder
1/2 t. salt
1 egg
1/2 c. chopped nuts

Cut dates into small pieces; add soda to boiling water. Pour over dates and let stand until cool. Cream oil or applesauce, honey and egg. Add dry ingredients and beat. Add date mixture and nuts and beat thoroughly. Fill custard cups 1/2 full that have been sprayed with a non-stick coating. Place in large flat pan; fill with water to within 1" of top of cups. Steam 30-45 minutes, until center is firm. Serve with Lemon Sauce.

Lemon Sauce:

1 c. warm water
2 T. cornstarch
1 t. vanilla
1 c. honey
1 T. butter
1 to 1 1/2 T. lemon juice

Place water in small saucepan. Whisk in cornstarch, then add remaining ingredients; cook over medium-high heat until thickened, about 3 minutes.

CREAMY "PUMPKIN" PIE

3 eggs
3/4 c. honey
2 T. light molasses
2 c. warm water
1/8 t. soda
1 t. salt
2/3 c. dry milk powder
1/4 t. powdered nutmeg
1/2 t. powdered ginger
1/4 t. powdered cloves
1/2 t. powdered cinnamon
2 c. mashed white beans

Blend all ingredients, adding in order given. When smooth, pour into chilled pastry-lined pan. Bake 10 minutes at 450°; reduce heat to 350° and bake 20-25 minutes, or until knife inserted in pie comes out clean.

CAROB CREAM PIE

2/3 c. hot water
1/4 c. malted milk powder
1/2 c. honey
2/3 c. carob powder
2 T. cornstarch
1/4 t. salt
1/2 t. cinnamon
1 T. vanilla
2 lb. tofu
1/3 c. butter or canola oil (opt.)

Blend water and first 4 ingredients until smooth, about 2 minutes. In 2 batches, blend all ingredients until smooth and creamy. Pour into unbaked 9" pie crust, Gluten-Free if desired, and bake about 35 minutes at 350° or until crust is done and filling is set.

COCONUT-OATMEAL CAKE

1 1/2 c. boiling water
1 c. oatmeal
1/2 c. canola oil or applesauce
2 eggs
1 1/2 c. wheat flour
1/2 c. white bean flour
1 1/2 c. honey
1/2 t. salt
1 t. baking powder
1 t. soda
1 t. cinnamon
1/2 c. shredded coconut

Pour water over oatmeal. Set aside to cool. Mix all other ingredients and pour into oat mixture; stir until evenly moistened.

Bake in 9"x13" cake pan that has been sprayed with a non-stick vegetable cooking spray at 350° for 35-40 minutes.

Frosting:

3/4 c. honey
3 T. milk
6 T. butter
2 T. molasses
1/2 c. chopped nuts
1 c. shredded coconut
1/4 c. dry Okara (opt.)

Bring honey, milk, butter and molasses to a full boil. Remove from heat. Add nuts, coconut and Okara. Spread on warm cake and place under broiler.

Bake just until frosting is bubbly and coconut is lightly browned.

PINTO BEAN-APPLE CAKE

1 c. honey
1/4 c. canola oil or applesauce
1 egg
*2 c. mashed pinto beans**
1 t. ginger
1 t. cinnamon
1/2 t. salt
1 t. soda
1 c. whole wheat or GF flour
2 T. white bean flour
1/2 t. cloves
1/2 t. allspice
2 t. vanilla
2 c. grated apples
1 c. raisins or dates
1 c. chopped nuts or seeds

*See Cooking Options Section for "Instant Mashed Beans."

Cream honey, oil or applesauce, egg and mashed beans. Add remaining ingredients and pour into 10" tube cake pan or 9"x13" cake pan that has been sprayed with a non-stick coating. Bake at 375° for 45 minutes.

GRANDPA'S CARROT CAKE

1/2 c. canola oil or applesauce
4 eggs
1 1/2 c. honey
1 c. finely diced dates
3 c. whole wheat or GF flour
1/2 c. white bean flour
1/2 t. allspice
1/2 t. salt
2 t. cinnamon
2 t. soda
5 c. finely grated carrots
1/2 c. shredded coconut

Combine and mix thoroughly oil or applesauce, eggs, honey, dates. Sift in flours, spices and salt. Stir in grated carrot. Place in 9"x13" baking dish that has been sprayed with a non-stick coating and bake at 350° for 40-45 minutes. Cool and sprinkle with powdered Sucanat* or frost with following:

Icing
4 oz. cream cheese
1/2 stick butter
1 t. vanilla
1 t. maple flavoring
1 c. dry non-instant milk
1/4 c. honey
*1 c. powdered Sucanat**
1 c. ea. walnut halves and coconut

Mix all together. Spread on cooked cake, adding a little water if necessary to make spreading easier. *See Cooking Options Section

RUTH'S HONEY SPONGE CAKE

1 1/2 c. honey
6 egg yolks
1 T. grated lemon peel
1/3 c. orange juice
1 t. vanilla
1/2 t. cloves
1 3/4 c. whole wheat or GF flour
1 T. white bean flour
6 egg whites
1 t. cream of tartar

Beat honey and egg yolks until creamy and thick (about 10 minutes). Add lemon peel, orange juice and vanilla. Add flours and beat well. Beat egg whites and cream of tartar until very stiff (at least 5 min.).

Fold into above mixture. Bake in ungreased angel food pan at 325° for 50 to 60 minutes, or until cake springs back from touch. Remove from oven and turn upside down to cool 2 hours before removing from pan.

Serve plain or with lemon or other fruit sauce.

Adapted from Natural Sweets and Treats, by Ruth Laughlin. (Out of Print)

NUTTY GINGERBREAD

3/4 c. honey
1/2 c. vegetable oil
(or 1/4 c. oil +1/4 c. applesauce)
1/2 c. light molasses
3 eggs
1 c. buttermilk
2 1/2 c. whole wheat flour
(OR, use 3 c. Rita's GF flour and omit bean flour.)
1/2 c. white bean flour
2 t. baking powder
1 t. baking soda
2 1/2 t. cinnamon
1 1/2 t. ginger
1 c. walnuts, coarsely chopped or 1 c. toasted sunflower seeds

Beat honey, oil or applesauce, eggs and molasses until creamy. Add remaining ingredients and mix until just moistened.

Pour into a 9"x13" baking dish that has been sprayed with a non-stick coating. Bake 35 to 40 minutes at 325°. Cut into 3" squares and serve with lemon sauce (p. 144) or applesauce.

RAISIN-NUT PINTO BEAN CAKE

1 c. honey
1/4 c. canola oil or applesauce
2 eggs
2 c. whole wheat or GF flour
1 T. white bean flour
1/2 t. salt
1 t. cinnamon
1 t. allspice
1/4 t. cloves
1 t. soda
2/3 c. applesauce
*2/3 c. mashed pinto beans**
1 c. raisins or dates
1 c. chopped nuts
1 t. vanilla
1 c. warm water

Cream honey and oil or applesauce, add eggs; beat until smooth. Combine dry ingredients, add alternately with vanilla and warm water. Add remaining ingredients. Pour into 9" square cake pans that have been sprayed with a non-stick coating. Bake 25 to 30 minutes at 375°. Cut into squares and dust with powdered sugar*. Adapted From The Queen's Kitchen. (Out of Print)

*See Options Section for "Instant Mashed Beans" and Powdered Sucanat.

SPICY PINTO CUPCAKES

Sift together:
2 c. whole wheat or GF flour
2 1/2 t. baking powder
1 1/4 c. honey
1 t. salt
1/2 t. allspice
1 t. cinnamon
1/2 t. cloves
3 T. dry milk powder
Add:
1/2 c. canola oil or applesauce
3/4 c. water
1 t. vanilla
1 T. molasses
1/2 t. grated orange rind
Beat 2 minutes.
Add:
2 eggs
1/4 c. water
1 T. dry milk powder
*3/4 c. mashed pinto or soy bean**

Beat 2 minutes more. Bake in cupcake pans that has been sprayed with a non-stick coating or papers at 375° for 20 minutes. Cool. Frost if desired. or sprinkle with powdered Sucanat*. Adapted From The Queen's Kitchen. (Out of Print)

*See Options Section for "Instant Mashed Beans" and Powdered Sucanat.

CANDIES USING DRY OKARA

Okara, the by product of making tofu, is a fluffy, high-fiber addition to these already nutritious candies. It is easy to make using only soaked beans, water, a blender, cheesecloth and ordinary cooking utensils.

See page 152 for "how-to" instructions on making Okara.

All recipes in this section are Gluten-Free.

OKARA ORANGE CRUNCH

Adapted from the famous Gluten Crunch Candy, this popular favorite is a nutritious addition to snacks and desserts. (The Amazing Wheat Book, by LeArta Moulton, see p. 183 for ordering information.)

1 c. dry Okara
1 c. shredded coconut
1 T. butter
2 T honey
1 capful orange extract

Melt butter and honey together. Mix all ingredients. Spread on cookie sheet and bake 10-15 minutes (or until browned and crispy) at 350°.

Stir occasionally to brown evenly.

CAROB CRACKLE

1 c. melted carob
2 c. Okara Orange Crunch

Carob may be melted in double boiler or in microwave. Stir in Okara Crunch, mixing thoroughly. Pour out on cookie sheet or wax paper and press flat with back of spoon.

Score with knife when cool. Place in freezer for 5 minutes if mixture sticks to pan. Store in refrigerator (if it lasts that long!).

MINTY SUNNYSEED SQUARES

3/4 c. melted honey
2 t. vanilla
1 c. non-instant dry milk powder
1 c. chunky peanut or almond butter
1/2 c. dry okara
1/4 c. toasted sunflower seeds
1/4 c. mint carob chips

Combine all but seeds and chips and mix well. Press into 9"x13" tray.

Cut into 1/2" squares and decorate with seeds and chips.

TOFU AND OKARA

SOYBEAN CURD (TOFU)

Tofu is an ideal high protein diet food, with 1/3 the calories as equal portions of eggs, 1/4-1/5 as much as beef. It contains most of the protein of the bean and is a versatile, easier-to-digest source of good quality protein than that found in meats. Cross-cultural studies seem to link use of vegetable proteins with the freedom from heart and circulatory diseases, as well as being much lower in fat. And all with NO CHOLESTEROL.

SOYBEAN MASH (OKARA)

Okara is the by-product of tofu. After soaked beans are blended and cooked with water, they are poured into a cloth which separates the bean residue from the soy milk. When all the milk has been extracted, a fluffy mash remains which retains some protein and LOTS of fiber. Okara is traditionally used as a meat extender in ground meat dishes, and as a substitute for wheat bran in baked goods. Use it in casseroles, stir fry, patties, loaves and breads.

SOY MILK

1 - Grind Whole Dry Beans ("Quick" method)

Grind 4 c. whole dry soybeans to a flour. Blend 1/2 c. flour with 3 c. hot water at a time. Skip to "Heat" instructions.

OR....

2 - Rinse, Soak and Grind (Traditional method)

Rinse 4 c. whole dry beans. Cover with 12 c. boiling water and let soak 3-4 hours. Drain and rinse in a colander. Blend 1 c. of beans and 3 cups fresh hot water at a time, not more than 1 minute, being careful not to grind too fine.

Heat

In a large (3-4 gallon) pan coated with cooking spray, bring mixture to a boil, reduce heat to medium low and cook, stirring occasionally, for 15 minutes.

If mixture starts to boil over, add a little cold water or remove from heat and reduce heat slightly.

Strain

In a large mixing bowl, set a colander lined with several layers of cheesecloth. Pour in soybean mixture, then wash out cooking pan and again coat with cooking spray. Set aside. Allow mixture to cool and drain 5 minutes.

Gather edges of cheesecloth and twist until cloth tightens, forming pulp into a ball. Lay twisted portion of cloth in center of ball and press with a wooden spoon (or your hands if you can stand the heat) to press out as much milk as possible. When pulp is fairly dry, open cloth and pour 3 c. boiling water over the pulp. (NOTE: this step is not necessary when using soy FLOUR.)

Repeat the pressing process, squeezing the ball with your hands as it cools to extract the most milk possible. The soy milk can be refrigerated and used in place of regular milk in almost any recipe.

The remaining pulp (Okara) can be refrigerated or dried and stored in air-tight containers and used as mentioned earlier.

HOMEMADE TOFU

Curdle

Again using your large pan coated with cooking spray, bring soy milk to a boil over high heat, stirring frequently, then reduce heat to medium and simmer for about 7 minutes. Remove pot from burner.

While simmering, dilute 1/2 c. of white vinegar or lemon juice (fresh, frozen or reconstituted) in 1 1/2 c. hot water. This is used as the coagulant. Stir soy milk vigorously and while stirring, pour in 1/3 of coagulant, stirring several more times to make sure solution is mixed in well. Now, stop stirring and hold stirring spoon upright in mixture and wait until mixture stops moving.

Lift out spoon. Sprinkle another 1/3 of coagulant over surface of milk, cover and let rest 5 minutes. This allows large, fluffy curds to form. If soy milk has completely curdled (mixture will be in the form of white curds and clear, pale yellow liquid), you are finished! If you still see milky liquid, gently stir the top part of the solution while adding remaining coagulant. Cover and let rest 3 more minutes.

Drain

Place cooking pot next to forming container lined with several layers of moistened cheesecloth. (You may use a specially made rectangular box with holes drilled into sides for drainage, or a colander.) Gently lower 8-10" strainer into curds and whey. This will allow you to ladle off whey from inside the strainer, without disturbing curds. When most whey is removed, remove strainer.

Gently ladle curds into forming container. Fold edges of cloth neatly over curds, place a lid or plate on top of cloth. If using a colander, the plate needs to be of a size that will not touch the sides of the colander as the mixture shrinks while draining and pressing.

On the top of the box lid or plate, place a 1 qt. jar of water and press for 15 minutes. For a firmer tofu, use a 2 qt. jar for 20-30 minutes. Turn container upside down and gently lower cheese into a bowl of cold water. In about 5-8 minutes, your tofu will be cool and firm.

Gently remove cloth and cut into 3" squares, or leave whole. Refrigerate in a container of water or wrap and freeze. Can be kept in fridge up to 1 week if water is changed every day or two. (Frozen tofu will have a more meat-like texture that is an excellent meat substitute, but don't expect a smooth, thawed tofu.)

COOKING OPTIONS

This section will answer many of your questions as well as give you some helpful hints to make nutritious meals more quickly.

ADDING BEAN FLOUR TO HOT SOUPS - **Option 1 -** Place bean flour and cool water in a small plastic container with a tight-fitting lid. Shake well to blend. Then add to hot soup mixture. **Option 2 -** Use a wire whisk to stir bean flour into hot liquid. For a creamier soup, sauce, or gravy, blend in small batches after soup has thickened.

COOKED, MASHED BEANS - If you mash cooked beans, you will end up with a fairly dry paste. Depending on the recipe, you may want to blend in a little cooking liquid or water to thin and fluff.

"INSTANT MASHED BEANS" - This thick mixture can be used in place of cooked, mashed beans in patties, loaves, casseroles, desserts, etc.

1 c. whole beans = approx. 1 1/8 c. bean flour.
1 c. water + 1/2 c. bean flour = 1 c. "instant mashed beans"
2 c. water + 3/4 c. bean flour = 2 1/2 c. fluffy mashed beans

To use instant mashed beans in dips and other recipes calling for cooked mashed beans, bring 1 c. water to a boil, then whisk in 1 c. bean flour mixed with 1 c. cool water. Cook and stir for 1 minute, until mixture thickens. Reduce heat to medium-low, cover pan and cook 4 minutes, stirring occasionally. This process produces a fairly stiff bean mixture similar to commercial canned refried beans. Add salt to taste.

For a fluffier bean mixture with a lighter, creamier texture which is better for dips, burrito and sandwich fillings, reduce bean flour to 3/4 c.

COOKED CRACKED BEANS - crack in hand or electric mill or heavy duty blender. Add 1 part beans and 2 parts water and bring to a boil. Cover and let sit 5 minutes. Put into strainer and drain.

Add water to cover and cook over medium heat for 15-20 minutes, until slightly tender, or add uncooked to any recipe that will be cooked for 20-30 minutes or more. OR, finely chop cooked beans.

COOKED CRACKED WHEAT - ***for fluffy cracked wheat to use in pilaf, patties, loaves, salads and sandwich fillings.*** Place 1 c. cracked wheat (with all flour particles sifted out) and 1 3/4 c. hot water in a small heavy saucepan. Bring mixture to a full boil. Cover with a tight-fitting lid, remove from heat, and let sit 15 minutes. Fluff with a fork. This can be refrigerated for 1 week, or frozen 6 months. **To freeze:** Place 1-2 cup portions in pint or quart zip-loc bags. Flatten as you press out air. Stack flat in freezer. To thaw, cover with hot water for 1-2 min.

FROZEN COOKED BEANS OR RICE - Freeze cooked beans or rice following directions above for freezing cracked wheat. Thaw in warm water to use in patties, loaves or casseroles, or add to soups 10 minutes before end of cooking time.

FASTER BAKING TIMES - *Expose more surface to heat for faster cooking time and less of your time and effort in the kitchen!*

If you are making **banana bread** or a **meatless loaf** that would be cooked in a loaf pan for 60 minutes, you can place mixture in muffin tins, custard cups, or in up to a 9"x13" pan and bake only 15-25 minutes. **Cake batter** to fill an 8" square pan makes a great bar or square when baked in a 9"x13" pan. **Breads** that would normally be baked in a loaf pan can be shaped into balls (use only 1 c. dough) and baked on cookie sheets to cut baking from 45 minutes to 25-30 minutes. **Casseroles** can be placed in custard cups or in a dish larger than the one called for. This will cut the baking time to about 15-25 minutes. **Cookies** can be baked as bars. Spread or spoon cookie dough 1/4" thick to edges of baking sheet. Bake until dough in center of pan is set.

Remember, *exposing more of the food's surface to heat speeds cooking time,* so spread out your ingredients in a larger pan or place them in individual-size small containers, rather than using one large, deep container.

FLAVORED SESAME OIL - found in Oriental section of grocery store. A medium-brown oil with the distinct flavor of toasted sesame seeds. A few drops per serving are used as a seasoning, NOT as a cooking oil.

POWDERED SUCANAT (dried cane juice) - In recipes where powdered sugar is called for, I use powdered Sucanat. Place 1 c. dry Sucanat granules in blender jar or food processor. Process at high speed until mixture is no longer grainy, stopping occasionally to scrape sugar from sides of jar. Mixture can be used like commercial powdered sugar.

******GLUTEN-FREE BAKED GOODS** - For those with wheat or gluten allergies or intolerances, this GF flour mixture can be mixed in advance and used in place of the wheat and bean flour called for in this book (and in most other baked goods). Adding extra protein in the form of eggs helps produce a lighter product.

Rita's Gluten Free Baking Mix

- 3 c. brown rice flour
- 1 c. tapioca flour
- 2/3 c. corn flour
- 1 T. xanthan gum
- 2 c. potato starch flour
- 1/2 c. soy or garbanzo bean flour
- 1/2 c. kidney bean flour (to give the flour a "brown" color)

Other excellent gluten-free flours are lentil, pea, amaranth, and quinoa. These flours can be found at your health food store... or grind your own!

HOME CANNING

BOTTLED BEANS, VEGETABLE MIXES AND BEAN SOUPS

With bottled beans, soups and other vegetable-bean mixtures, you have ready-to-eat meals in any emergency - like "Oops, it's dinner time already!" With pre-cooked beans already to add to a main dish, or soups ready to heat and serve, **most meals can be ready to eat in 30 minutes or less, from first step to first bite.** *To ensure safe canning, recipes in the first section have been developed using guidelines from the 32nd edition of the Ball Blue Book.*

All recipes in this section are Gluten-Free.

BOTTLED BEANS - DRIED KIDNEY, ETC.

Use kidney or any other variety of dried beans or dried peas. Cover washed, sorted beans or peas with cold water. Let stand 12 to 18 hours in a cool place. Drain and rinse. OR, cover washed, sorted beans with hot water. Bring to a boil and cook 2 minutes; cover and remove from heat. Let sit 1 hour; drain and rinse.

After preparing beans using one of the above methods, add hot water to cover and boil 30 minutes. Pack hot into hot jars, leaving 1-inch head space. Add 1/2 teaspoon salt to each pint or 1 teaspoon salt to each quart. (I usually substitute bouillon or vegetable soup base OR add only half the salt.)

Cover with cooking water, leaving 1-inch head space. Remove air bubbles. Adjust caps. Process pints 1 hour and 15 minutes, quarts 1 hour and 30 minutes at 10 pounds pressure. (See processing pressure chart on page 160.)

Note: *By bottling 1 pressure canner holding 7 quart jars 5 days per week for 1 month, you could have 140 quarts of ready-to-eat beans. They can be served plain or to increase the nutrient and fiber content of almost everything you eat.*

BOTTLED BEAN SOUPS

HOT RED BEAN SOUP

18 c. soaked kidney beans (9 c. dry)
3 c. chopped onions
hot water to cover
1 T. chicken or vegetable base per qt.
2 hot red peppers, chopped
or 1 to 1 1/2 t. tabasco sauce

Place all ingredients in large saucepan with water to cover; bring to boiling. Pour hot into hot jars, leaving 1-inch head space. Adjust caps.

Process pints 1 hour and 15 minutes, quarts 1 hour and 30 minutes at 10 pounds pressure. Yield: about 7 qt.

TOMATO VEGETABLE SOUP

6 c. water
4 c. chopped tomatoes
6 c. cubed potatoes
3 qt. cut corn, uncooked
2 c. chopped onions
2 c. diced celery
1 qt. sliced carrots
1 qt. soaked Navy beans
7 T. chicken or vegetable soup base

Place all ingredients in large pan and boil for 5 minutes. Ladle hot into jars, leaving 1-inch head space. Adjust caps. Process pints 1 hour, quarts 1 hour and 15 minutes at 10 pounds pressure. Yield: about 7 quarts.

VEGETABLE BEAN SOUP

6 c. water
6 c. chopped tomatoes
4 c. cubed potatoes
8 c. cut corn, uncooked
2 c. shredded cabbage
2 c. chopped onions
1 c. chopped green bell pepper
4 c. sliced carrots
5 c. soaked kidney beans
3-4 T. chicken or vegetable soup base

Place all ingredients in large pan and boil for 5 minutes. Ladle hot into jars, leaving 1-inch head space. Adjust caps. Process pints 1 hour, quarts 1 hour and 15 minutes at 10 pounds pressure. Yield: about 7 quarts.

SPLIT PEA SOUP

6 c. dried split peas
6 qt. water
4 1/2 c. sliced carrots
3 c. chopped onion
1/2 t. celery seed, powdered
1/8 t. garlic powder
1/2 t. pepper
5-6 T. chicken or vegetable soup base

Combine dried peas and water; bring to a boil, reduce heat and simmer, covered, about 1 hour or until peas are soft. For a smooth soup, blend and return to pot. Add remaining ingredients and simmer gently about 30 minutes. If mixture is too thick, more water may be added. Pour hot into hot jars, leaving 1-inch head space. Adjust caps. Process points 1 hour and 15 minutes, quarts 1 hour and 30 minutes at 10 pounds pressure. Yield: about 7 qt.

VEGETABLE BEAN SOUPS

Recipes in this section have been developed using the guidelines found in the 1990 Updated Home Canning Guide, adapted from USDA's Complete Guide To Home Canning, Ag Info. Bulletin #539.

For the following Vegetable Soups, fill hot jars 1/2 full with solids, then to 1" from top with cooking liquid. Adjust caps. In all cases, process pints 60 minutes and quarts 75 minutes.

ALTITUDE	PROCESSING PRESSURES
0 - 2,000 ft.	10 lb.
2,001 ft - 4,000 ft.	12 lb.
4,001 - 6,000	13 lb.
6,001+	14 lb.

"CLAM" 'N BEAN SOUP

9 c. soaked white beans
4 c. chopped or shredded potatoes
20 c. boiling water
3 T. chopped pimientos
1/2 c. chopped green pepper
5-7 T. clam base (to taste)

Bring all ingredients to a boil and cook 5 minutes. Fill hot jars halfway with vegetable mixture. Fill jars with liquid, leaving 1" headspace. Adjust lids. Process as outlined above*. Makes 7 qt.

COUNTRY VEGETABLE SOUP

5 c. soaked white beans
2 c. sliced or diced potatoes
2 c. sliced or diced carrots
2 c. chopped onions
2 1/2 c. sliced celery
1/2 c. shredded cabbage
20 c. water or bean liquid
2 T. Country Blend All Purpose Seas. *(see p. 65)*
1/2 t. salt per quart (opt.)

Bring all ingredients to a boil and cook 5 minutes. Fill hot jars halfway with vegetable mixture. Fill jars with liquid, leaving 1" headspace. Adjust lids. Process as outlined above*. Makes 7 qt.

GREAT CHILI SOUP

12 c. tomato juice
6 c. hot water
1 1/2 c. chopped green peppers
1 1/2 c. diced onions
12 c. soaked kidney, pinto or red beans
6 t. chicken or vegetable soup base
2 t. salt (opt.)
5 T. chili powder
1 t. ground cumin

Bring all ingredients to a boil and cook 5 minutes. Fill hot jars halfway with bean mixture. Fill jars with liquid, leaving 1" headspace. Adjust lids. Process as outlined on page 160. Makes 7 qt.

NEW ENGLAND "CLAM" CHOWDER

1 c. chopped onions
5 c. diced or grated potatoes
20 c. boiling water
1 T. dried parsley
3 c. diced or grated carrots
3 c. chopped celery
2 c. soaked lima or white beans
pepper to taste
5-7 T. clam base, to taste

Bring all ingredients to a boil and cook 5 minutes. Fill hot jars halfway with bean mixture. Fill jars with liquid, leaving 1" headspace. Adjust lids. Process as outlined on page 160. Makes 7 qt. For "real" clam chowder, add 3 1/2 c. chopped clams and process 100 minutes.

MANHATTAN "CLAM" CHOWDER

1 bay leaf
1/2 t. thyme
1 T. dried parsley
1/2 t. crushed basil leaves
4 c. diced potatoes
5 c. bottled tomatoes
2 c. chopped celery
1 c. soaked lima beans
2 c. diced carrots
1 c. chopped onion
20 c. boiling water
5-7 T. clam base, to taste

Bring all ingredients to a boil and cook 5 minutes. Fill hot jars halfway with bean mixture. Fill jars with liquid, leaving 1" headspace. Adjust lids. Process as outlined on page 160. Makes 7 qt. For "real" clam chowder, add 3 1/2 c. chopped clams and process 100 minutes.

POTATO BEAN SOUP

20 c. boiling water
2 c. chopped celery
1 c. diced or shredded carrots
2 qt. diced or shredded potatoes
2 c. chopped onions
1 c. soaked blackeyes
5 T. chicken or vegetable soup base
1 T. dried parsley
1/2 t. pepper (opt.)

Bring all ingredients to a boil and cook 5 minutes. Fill hot jars halfway with bean mixture. Fill jars with liquid, leaving 1" headspace. Adjust lids. Process as outlined on page 160. Makes 7 qt.

BOTTLED VEGETABLES FOR SOUPS

These versatile combinations make excellent soups. Just open, add additional water and flavoring (thickening if desired) and serve! Or add dumpling batter, cooked pasta or cooked grains just before serving.

To serve: To 1 qt. vegetables and liquid, add 2 c. liquid (water, milk or unsalted vegetable cooking liquid).

To thicken: Whisk 3 T. cornstarch or 1/3 c. white bean flour into slightly warm soup. Bring to a boil and cook 3 minutes.

To add pasta or grains: To 2 c. boiling water, add 1 c. dry noodles, 1/2 c. cracked wheat or brown rice. Bring back to a boil. Cover and remove from heat. Let rest 15 minutes. Add to cooked soup.

To Process: For the following **Vegetable For Soups,** fill hot jars to 1" from top with vegetables and cooking liquid. In all cases, bouillon or soup base is optional. For a salt restricted diet, look for no-salt seasonings. Adjust caps. *In all cases,* process pints 75 minutes and quarts 90 minutes, using the previous altitude chart for processing pressure. Each vegetable combination makes approximately 7 quarts.

HARVEST SPECIAL

6 c. sliced carrots
6 c. cut, whole kernel sweet corn
6 c. cut green beans
6 c. shelled or soaked lima beans
4 c. crushed tomatoes
4 c. diced zucchini
9 T. chicken or vegetable soup base

Process as outlined on page 160.

VEGETABLE MUSHROOM

3 c. shredded cabbage
8 c. sliced celery
5 c. diced carrots
6 c. coarsely shredded potatoes
5 c. soaked pinto or black beans
2 c. cut, whole kernel sweet corn
4 c. sliced mushrooms
9 T. chicken or clam soup base

Process as outlined on page 160.

CRUCIFEROUS SOUP

Cancer-fighting vegetables from the cabbage family, combined with heart-healthy beans for protein and fiber.

10 c. shredded cabbage
7 c. sliced cauliflower pcs.
7 c. broccoli stems and tops
4 c. sliced carrots
2 c. soaked kidney beans
2 c. soaked garbanzo beans
9 T. chicken or vegetable soup base

Process as outlined on page 160.

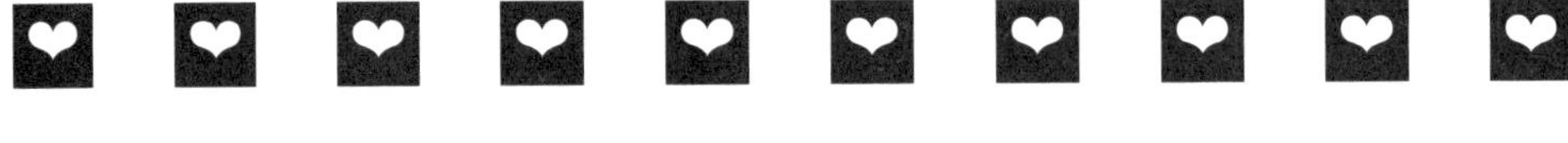

INFORMATION SECTION

(WHY BEANS???)

The topics we hear most about these days are CHOLESTEROL, FAT, FIBER, and PROTEIN.

Do we have enough, too little or too much? WHY BE CONCERNED AT ALL?

GLUTEN INTOLERANCE - How to convert recipes

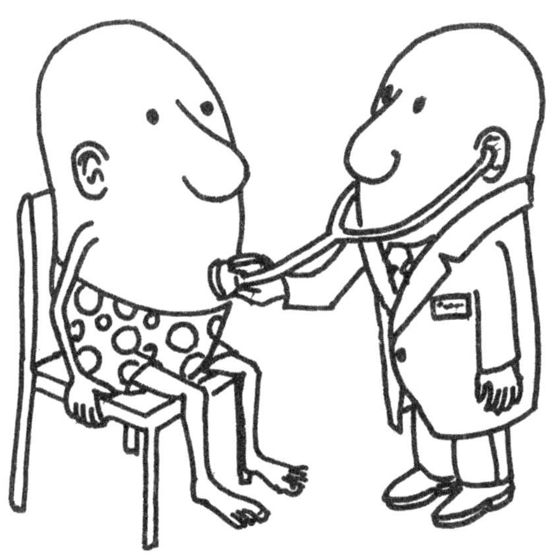

10% FAT DIETS REVERSE HEART DISEASE...as well as nearly all other diseases

According to the most recent research of Dr. Dean Ornish, a diet containing less than 10% fat *reverses heart disease.* A low-fat vegetarian diet, together with a program for dealing with stress, has been responsible for reversal of heart disease in *82%* of his patients. Dr. Ornish also says "The benefits of our program are not confined to heart disease, but may apply to other illnesses as well." I heartily agree with his thinking (as do a growing number of health professionals) and believe that when we feed our bodies nourishing foods, we are not as susceptible to most of the common ailments so prevalent in our society.

Along with proper foods, Dr. Ornish recommends exercise and stress management, as these play an important part in any total-health program. Lest you be led to believe that you can eat your way thin, that is only partially true. To be truly healthy, you must pay attention to *all* your body's needs.

Dr. Ornish also suggests that a modified program be followed as preventive therapy. This program is less stringent, and is aimed at gradually reducing fat and cholesterol consumption until the cholesterol level falls to 150. ***Your body will function best and you will feel your best if you follow a total-health program in which only 10 to 20 percent of the calories are supplied by fat and which emphasizes the use of whole grains, beans (legumes) and vegetables.***

MOST BEANS, GRAINS,VEGETABLES ARE ONLY 2-3% FAT

Just think what your life would be like if you could eat satisfying meals, lose excess weight, *never* count another calorie, and never be fat again! The secret lies in beans, grains and other vegetable sources, nearly all of which contain **only 2-3% fat!** You can even *add* oils to some recipes without going above even the 10% fat level recommended by Dr. Ornish and others.

Soybeans and garbanzo beans are higher in fat than other beans, making them much more filling. We *need* a small amount of fat (preferably from vegetable sources) each day to maintain proper cell function, so high-fat vegetables (like avocados, olives) and beans like soy and garbanzo *should* be included in your meal planning if you are not eating meat.

WHAT ABOUT CHOLESTEROL?

Did you know that beans can help lower your cholesterol level? Not only do they contain NO cholesterol, "they actually help the body get rid of what are considered *bad* cholesterol cells" (LDL's). *"Recent studies have shown that by adding beans to a low cholesterol diet, you can lower your cholesterol level by as much as 15 to 20 percent.* The reason for this is in the high concentration of soluble fiber in beans. This soluble fiber has a cleaning affect on the body's arteries." (California Dry Bean Advisory Board)

THE FIBER–CHOLESTEROL CONNECTION

"Fiber, most broadly, is the portion of plant foods our bodies can't digest. It comes in two basic categories — insoluble and soluble. Insoluble fibers, which *don't* dissolve in water, are the more obviously "fibrous" of the two. These include the woody or structural parts of plants, such as fruit and vegetable skins and the bran coating around wheat and corn kernels. They pass through the digestive tract largely unchanged and speed the passage of whatever else comes along for the ride.

"Soluble fibers, which *do* dissolve in water, are found in abundance in beans, oats, barley, broccoli, prunes, apples, and citrus fruits. They have the consistency of gels and tend to slow the passage of material through the digestive tract.

The process of refining foods removes much of the insoluble fiber — hence the widespread NEED for bran and other fiber supplements and laxatives. Research has shown that cultures which eat whole foods have no need for extra fiber, nor do those cultures suffer the health problems caused from the lack of adequate fiber."

How much fiber is enough?

British physician Denis Burkitt found that the rural Africans he studied ate some 50 to 150 grams of fiber a day. Americans, by contrast, typically consume about 20 grams. It is generally accepted by many researchers today that we should double or triple our fiber intake (mainly soluble fibers, eaten as unrefined foods) and cut our fat consumption at least by one half. To increase soluble fiber intake, we could eat 1 3/4 c. of DRY oatmeal per day. Or, how about 2/3 c. of DRY oat bran, 3 standard doses of Metamucil, Fiberall, or other over-the-counter bulk laxatives? *One cup of beans would provide the same amount of fiber, but would be much more pleasant to eat and could be prepared with an endless variety of tastes.*

Since beans, peas and lentils are one of the richest sources of fiber and an excellent source of protein with almost no fat, they are the *stars of today* as well as tomorrow. Modern technology and research is helping to prove that the foods we refine are often the very ones we should be eating in unrefined form.

Increasing fiber foods has the effect of lowering cholesterol - in some cases dramatically. Also important, however, is cutting back on cholesterol-rich foods. This can easily be accomplished by replacing several "meat meals" each week with beans, peas, lentils and whole grains.

Fiber in Baby Foods

Refined cereals, fruits and vegetables are often the cause of constipation in infants. To remedy this, bean flour can be cooked in a dry saucepan, microwave or oven until slightly browned. These flours will then cook in only 1 minute, when added to water. By adding reconstituted, cooked bean flours (seasoned to taste) to cereals, vegetables and even fruits, infants and children can be fed meals which are more nutritious and unlikely to cause constipation. Brown rice flour is also excellent to add to foods for children.

Soy milk, used in many formulas, can be made at home and added to many foods for children, especially cereals. See the section on Tofu and Okara for homemade soy milk.

Fiber in Gluten-Free Diets (Celiacs)

Until recently, it was believed that celiacs should avoid fiber, specifically grains. Now, with patience, even those with damaged digestive systems can use white rice flour and finely ground bean, pea, and lentil flours, gradually working up to using brown rice flour. Those with extreme sensitivities should grind their own flours or check to be sure the commercially ground flours are milled in a wheat-, corn-, oats-, barley- and rye-free environment. Since beans, peas, and lentils contain soluble fiber, they do not have the **scouring effect** of grains, and are generally well tolerated.

NUTRITION - IN A HURRY!

Beans and Bean flour added to soups, breads and other foods helps create a much more nutritious meal. Beans are an excellent source of protein, forming a complete protein when combined with rice, corn and many other foods. In today's fast-paced world, we need super-nutritious foods to keep us going and using bean flours, those foods can be prepared super-fast!

***See the "Introduction to Natural Foods" section in the *new* "*Natural* Meals In Minutes," also by Rita Bingham, with easy, fast, low fat recipes for breads, cakes, cookies, cereals, soups, salads, sandwich fillings, patties, loaves... and MORE!

This book is a combination of the first three "*Natural* Meals" booklets covering cooking with basic natural foods, sprouting and fat-free 3-minute cheeses. Each recipe also contains a nutritional analysis to quickly analyze your dietary intake.

PROTEIN

Legumes Provide A More Usable Protein

Although legumes contain smaller quantities of body building protein than do meats and dairy products, plant proteins are more readily used by the body than are animal proteins. Dr Lendon Smith, author of Feed Your Kids Right, states **"A six-ounce steak will provide 700 calories and only about 30 grams of usable protein. Two and a half cups of cooked beans will provide the same number of calories and yet deliver 50 percent *more* usable protein."** According to the Idaho/Washington Dry Pea & Lentil Commissions, **lentils provide 112 grams of protein per pound, as compared with eggs at 36 grams per pound!**

How much protein is enough?

Research has shown that any excess protein is converted into carbohydrates; then, if not burned as energy, it converts to fat, just as if you ate an extra slice of chocolate cake. That is one good reason to monitor closely the protein intake from all sources. When using concentrated sources of protein, like milk, cheese, tofu and gluten, it is still possible to eat too much protein. Many medical authorities now suggest we eat less protein, regardless of the source.

George Beinhorn, in Bike World Magazine, states: "The United States Government's own 70-gram recommendation was established on the basis of research that clearly showed 30 grams to be completely adequate. The extra 40 grams were labeled a 'margin of safety.' Though one Food and Nutrition board member reported that the real reason behind the high figure was that the board feared a 'public outcry' over the 30 gram figure."

The National Academy of Sciences' recent anti-cancer report warns that Americans are eating too much meat, too much protein (especially animal protein) and too much fat. The report recommends we reduce all dietary fats by 25%. (Other researchers insist it must be cut by 75% for noticeable improvement.) That includes meat, dairy products, vegetable fats and shortening. About 40% of the calories in a typical American diet is derived from fats. A dramatic reduction is urged upon us now because it is found that most Americans consume 200% to 400% more protein than needed, resulting in serious health abnormalities. How to Save Big Money Grocery and Household Shopping, by Jil Abegg.

Excess Protein Consumption

Some of the health abnormalities related to excessive protein consumption are: heart disease, arteriosclerosis, premature aging, mental illness, mineral imbalances (causing severe calcium and magnesium deficiencies, as well as deficiencies in vitamins B6 and B3). Sources include U. S. Army Medical Research and Nutrition Laboratory, Dr. Lennart Krook, and Dr. Uri Nikolayev, as well as doctors from Holland and Denmark.

The National Academy of Science urges us to replace the fattier animal protein with low-fat plant protein, such as dried beans, peas, lentils, soybeans and soybean products.

Complete and Incomplete Proteins

Plant protein comes from three classes of foods: legumes and vegetables, seeds, and grains. Protein from plant sources are "incomplete proteins," because one or more of the eight essential amino acids are missing or in short supply (with the exception to soybeans). Dry beans belong to the legumes class, along with dry peas, lentils and peanuts.

As stated earlier, in order for the protein in dry beans to become complete, beans must be combined with another protein source, from another class of foods, such as seeds and grains (or dairy products). Legumes are born mixers as well as meat extenders. Cooked beans (still firm) can be chopped or coarsely ground and mixed with ground meats to stretch your dollar and improve nutrition. A meal containing legumes and seeds, legumes and grains, or seeds and grains provides complete protein needed for health and growth. Legumes and grains, etc. eaten as much as 2 days apart will still combine properly, as the body extracts and stores the amino acids from the beans and combines them into proteins as a variety of foods are eaten.

Note: Beans are classed with vegetables, so combining vegetables with seeds or vegetables with grains would also form a complete protein.

According to information obtained from Brigham Young University agronomy department, beans mixed with grains form a high quality complete protein that can be tolerated by people of all ages, even infants, if adequate breast milk is not available. For babies, mix *1/4 c. very fine millet or brown rice flour* with *2 T. any kind very fine bean flou*r and *1 cup water for cereal, 2 cups water for formula.*

Soybeans as a source of protein

Soybeans contain all the amino acids necessary to form a complete protein, equal to that of animal proteins. Most often, grocery stores carry soybeans in the form of canned, cooked beans, or Tofu, a versatile product that can be used in almost *everything* you eat or cook.

HIGH IN B VITAMINS, CARBOHYDRATES AND IRON

Dry beans also supply important amounts of B vitamins that help turn food into energy and keep digestive and nervous systems healthy. In addition, they contain "working calorie" carbohydrates which digest slowly and satisfy hunger longer. In the minerals category, they supply iron-building red blood, calcium and phosphorus for strong bones and teeth, and potassium for regulating body fluid balance. "A Bean for all Seasons" published by The Baby Lima Council of California.

FLATULENCE (GAS)

"It is a well established fact that the production of flatulence is associated with consumption of legume seeds. The raffinose sugars which are contained in beans are the cause of gas production. These sugars contain three or more simple sugars (sucrose contains two). The digestive enzymes in the gastrointestinal tract are not capable of breaking these sugars apart into simple sugars for absorption so they pass into the colon. In the lower intestine, the sugars are metabolized by bacteria and form carbon dioxide, hydrogen and methane gas.

Because of the soluble fibers found in abundance in beans, they tend to slow the passage of material through the digestive tract. This means that even though gas may be produced, beans usually travel slowly, without causing diarrhea often present when an abundance of grain or bran is consumed.

Sprouting Helps Reduce Gas

"According to recent research at Utah State University, germination (sprouting) or fermentation of the beans reduce the amount of complex sugars and consequently the gas production. Cooking has little effect on the raffinose sugars and flatulence." "Dry Beans & Peas", Georgia Lauritzen, Cooperative Extension Service, Logan, UT.

Beans that are first sprouted, then cooked are more easily tolerated. Many have verified that the *regular* inclusion of small amounts of a variety of beans in their diet (at least 2-3 times per week) helped their tolerances increase.

A friend reported that she helped plan and serve a group dinner at which everything served was made from whole grains and whole beans. Plates were piled high with delicious looking and tasting samples. Those eating the meal were unused to whole foods, especially grains and beans. The next day, she called around to see if anyone had experienced any "digestive difficulties." *No one had!* The reason - *all grains and beans were first sprouted before being prepared into the wide variety of appetizing dishes. The moral* - SPROUT, and include plenty of fresh, uncooked sprouts along with your favorite cooked sprout dishes.

Beano®

Beano® is an enzyme, now packaged in tablets which should be taken with beans (or any gassy foods) each time you eat them. This enzyme seems to help eliminate the gas for many people who have used the product. Beano® is available in health stores and most grocery stores.

Discarding soak water

Also helpful is to discard the soaking water when beans are soaked overnight. When using the quick-soak method, discard the water used when boiling for 2 minutes and then soaking for 1 hour. When using beans that have been cracked, discard boiling water used after soaking for 5 minutes.

Regular Consumption

OR, for the simplest solution of ALL, just give your digestive system a chance to get used to beans by consuming them in small quantities at first and gradually increasing your intake. Your system WILL develop the friendly bacteria needed to digest them as well as any other high fiber food. Starting with sprouted peas, lentils and mung beans, the mildest of the legumes, will help your system adjust more quickly.

Bean Flours

Beans ground to a fine flour can be added in small quantities to nearly everything you cook . Beans in this form seem to be easier to digest since they require no chewing. Also, using beans in small quantities *regularly* is the easiest way to help your digestive system develop the enzymes necessary to digest beans efficiently. Bean flours are used in baked goods made from your regular recipes in combination with other flours, or as cream soups, sauces, dips or in loaves, patties or casseroles. ***Bean flours provide the fastest and easiest way to prepare bean meals.***

Stone Ground Bean, Pea and Lentil flours can be ordered directly from Bob's Red Mill at 5209 S. E. International Way, Milwaukie, OR 97222, or phone (503) 654-3215, fax (503) 653-1339. You may request a mail order catalog or the name of a Red Mill distributor near you. Also available is a new Gift Pack containing four 24 oz. packages of your choice of Bean, Pea or Lentil Flours. Each package includes recipes. Flours available are Black, Pinto, Garbanzo and White Bean, Green Pea and Red Lentil.

BEANS IN HISTORY

Simple Foods and Better Health

Throughout history, many people have experienced improved health when they were forced to live on more simple, basic foods; their health improved and they were even able to feel better while eating smaller quantities of food. One reason for their improved health is that commercially prepared foods are almost always filled with chemical additives, colorings, flavorings, and depleted of the unstable part of the food that allows it to spoil. Whole foods should always be our *first* choice, since foods in their more natural state are more easily utilized by our bodies.

Poor Man's Meat

Dry beans are among the oldest of important staple foods and have long been known for their low cost and high nutritional value. Often called "poor man's meat," a pound of beans, when cooked, will make about 9 servings, compared to 5 servings per pound of cheese and up to 4 servings per pound of meat, poultry or fish.

24 Carat Meals

Beans were once considered to be worth their weight in gold — the jeweler's "carat" owes its origin to a pea-like bean on the east coast of Africa. They also once figured very prominently in politics. During the age of the Romans, balloting was done with beans. White beans represented a vote of approval and the dark beans meant a negative vote. "How to Buy DRY BEANS, PEAS, and LENTILS," U. S. Department of Agriculture.

The use of beans dates back to as long ago as 7000 B.C., with the remains of lentils being found in the Egyptian tombs dating back more than four thousand years. Soybeans and mung beans have always been highly regarded by the people of China and India. In Cuba, the black bean is a favorite. Mexico favors all sizes of kidney beans. Navy beans, cranberry beans and white beans are most popular in the New England states. The South and Southwest prefer red beans, pinto beans and black-eyed peas. With this rich heritage of ideas and the availability of such a wide variety of beans, we can enjoy beans of a variety of flavors, colors and a multitude of ethnic seasonings.

BEANS IN THE KITCHEN OF TODAY

Cooked Beans

Cooked, mashed beans can be added to soups, sauces, patties, loaves, casseroles, "meat" pies, sandwich fillings, dips, etc. Dry beans can be soaked, cooked and frozen, or soaked and pressure bottled. I use both methods, but prefer bottled beans as they are the fastest to prepare and the easiest to use. Also, they taste most like the canned beans available at the grocery store.

Cream Soups and Sauces

ALL cooked beans can be pureéd to make "almost instant" cream soups or soup base, and can be served as a "cup-a-soup" for a quick, high protein meal in minutes. They need no added fats to make them creamy, rich and thick.

Grinding Bean Flour

*******When added to boiling water, bean flours thicken in only 1 minute, and in 3 minutes are ready to eat. Bean flours added to baked goods increase vitamins and minerals and provide a source of complete protein.***

Modern equipment for the kitchen has revolutionized the use of beans! Dry beans can be ground to a fine flour using a hand grinder for small quantities, or electric mills for larger quantities. Bean flour stores for up to 6 months on the shelf, 1 year under refrigeration, and is great to have on hand for "instant" soups, sauces, dips, sandwich fillings and gravies, and to add to almost everything you cook or bake.

There are several electric home mills which are guaranteed to grind all types of grains and beans to a flour as fine as wheat flour. These are the K-Tec Kitchen Mill, NutriMill, UltraMill, and the GrainMaster Whisper Mill. Hand mills will also grind grains and beans to a flour, although not quite as fine. Mills with grinding stones must be cleaned after each 2 cups of beans by grinding 1 cup of hard wheat. Do not grind soy beans if your mill uses grinding stones. If beans are too large to go easily into the grinding chamber of your electric mill, crack first with a blender or hand grain cracker.

Sort beans, checking for broken, dirty beans or rock pieces. (Most beans nowdays have been "triple cleaned," making this step unnecessary.) Pour into hopper of your mill. I like to place the mill in my kitchen sink to eliminate most of the bean dust from grinding. Set mill to grind on medium-fine. The resulting flour should be as fine as the wheat flour used in baking breads, cookies, etc. (A small electric seed or coffee mill, or heavy-duty blender can be used, but will produce a more coarse flour.) Turn on mill and begin (if necessary) stirring beans where they go into the grinding chamber (with the handle of a spoon) so they will not get stuck. This is not necessary in some mills or for smaller beans or for peas and lentils. Sponge filter should be cleaned after each 2 cups of beans in the K-Tec. (Or, keep an extra filter on hand.) If flour is being thrown from mill, cover mill with a large kitchen towel, leaving a small opening for stirring beans.

Beans which have absorbed excess moisture will cause caking on electric mill parts. Thoroughly brush away flour residue from mill after each use. (I like to use a clean, stiff paint brush.) Then run 1 cup of dry grain through the mill to clean out internal parts. Store flour in an air tight container, preferably in the refrigerator if not used within several weeks.

BUYING AND STORING BEANS

In addition to being good for our health, beans are also good for our food budget. So let's get started! Beans are *so* inexpensive that you can afford to buy and store several varieties at first, adding more to your pantry as you learn more ways to use them. They have been called "the world's most versatile staple food."

Check the quality of beans before you buy. They should be clean, bright colored and uniform in size with no visible damage. Cracked or chipped beans indicate a low quality product. Federal or State graded packages have been graded as to size, color, and foreign matter. Many times, field run beans contain dirt and rocks and must be more carefully cleaned before using.

Dry beans will keep indefinitely if stored below 70° F. in a tightly covered container in a dry place. Do not keep dry beans in the refrigerator, as the moisture they absorb will adversely affect cooking times. High temperature and humidity, as well as age, lengthen the cooking time, so rotate your storage.

Store up to 125 pounds of assorted beans per person. The amount depends on how many fruits and vegetables are stored (fresh, frozen, bottled, dehydrated). The Benson Institute, Brigham Young University, Provo, Utah 84602, suggests that each person requires approximately 1 lb. fruits or vegetables (including beans) per day.

MOST COMMON VARIETIES

BLACK BEANS (Turtle Beans) are small and black, but turn a rich, mahogany brown when cooked. They can be used in soups, loaves, patties and in Oriental and Mediterranean dishes.

BLACKEYE PEAS are small, oval-shaped and creamy white with a black spot on one side. They cook more quickly than most beans and are reputed to cause less gas. They are used primarily as a main dish vegetable. (They are really *beans*, not peas, but the name is used in some regions of the country.)

GARBANZO BEANS are also known as "chick peas," are nut-flavored and are commonly pickled in vinegar and oil for salads. In their "unpickled" form, they can be served as a main dish vegetable, or mashed and used as a binding agent in loaves and patties.

GREAT NORTHERN BEANS are large, white beans used in soups, salads, casserole dishes, and baked bean dishes.

KIDNEY BEANS are large and have a red color and kidney shape. They are popular for chili con carne and add color and body to salads and many Mexican dishes.

LIMA BEANS are white, broad and flat, and come in a variety of sizes. They are not widely known as dry beans, but make an excellent main dish vegetable and can also be used in soups and casseroles.

MUNG BEANS are usually served as long, succulent sprouts in Oriental dishes and at salad bars. They are small, green, and slightly oval in shape. They can easily be sprouted at home and used as crunchy sprouts in salads and stir fry. They can also be cooked whole and used in place of any bean.

NAVY BEANS include Great Northern, pea, flat small white and small white beans. They are very versatile and can be used in any recipe calling for beans.

PEA BEANS are small, oval and white. They are a favorite for home baked beans, soups and casseroles. They hold their shape well when cooked.

PINTO BEANS are of the same species as the kidney and red beans. Beige-colored and speckled, they are used mainly in salads and chili.

RED AND PINK BEANS, related to the kidney bean, are used in many Mexican dishes and chili. Pink beans have a more delicate flavor than red beans.

SOYBEANS are the "king" of beans when it comes to protein. Ounce for ounce, the soybean contains twice as much protein as meat, four times that of eggs, twelve times that of milk. It is the only bean than is a complete protein and is loaded with vitamins A, B, C, E, minerals and lecithin. Soybeans can also be sprouted under pressure, as are Mung Beans, to be used in oriental cooking.

Dry Peas and Lentils

GREEN DRY PEAS have a distinct flavor and are usually made into a thick soup which can be made from whole or split peas. In Europe, many chefs used powdered beans and peas to thicken soups as well as to add a rich flavor.

YELLOW DRY PEAS have a less pronounced flavor than other types and is in demand in the Southern and Eastern parts of the country, as well as in many other countries of the world.

DRY SPLIT PEAS are used mainly for split pea soup. However, they combine well with many different foods. Pea flour can be used in the same ways as Dry Whole Peas. Specially grown whole peas are dried and their skins are removed by a special machine. Another machine then breaks the peas in half. Since Split Peas do not have a protective skin, they will not store as well as whole peas.

DRY WHOLE PEAS are used in making soups, casseroles, patties and croquettes, vegetable side dishes, dips and appetizers.

LENTILS are an old world legume with a peppery taste and are disc-shaped, about the size of a pea. They are the easiest and fastest to cook (30 minutes with no advance preparation) since they require no soaking. Like soybeans, they are a complete protein and are also rich in iron and B vitamins. They can be served raw, (as sprouts) or cooked and used in making soups, casseroles, patties and croquettes. (They are also excellent sprouted and used raw in salads. See instructions below.)

SPROUTING DRY BEANS

Wash and sort beans; place in large bowl with 6 cups of water per pound of beans. Let stand overnight, or at least 12 hours. Drain and rinse, then put beans into a sprouting container.

To sprout in a quart jar, measure 1 cup of soaked beans and cover with a piece of nylon net secured with a rubber band or jar ring, or use a commercial sprouting lid. *In a sprouting tray* (a tray with a plastic or metal bottom which acts as a strainer), cover with a layer that is 2 or 3 beans thick.

Cover and place in a warm area (around 70° F), rinsing and draining at least 2 times a day with warm water. *The rinsing and draining is the most important of the sprouting process.* Tip jar of beans upside down and at an angle to drain until no water drips from jar. For trays, tip at an angle after rinsing, until no water drips from tray. Within 2 days most fresh seeds will have sprouted as long as the seed. Older seeds may take as long as 5 days. Be sure to rinse and drain thoroughly, as older seeds easily become slimy.

CONVERTING RECIPES TO GLUTEN-FREE

Celiacs and those allergic or sensitive to wheat, oats, barley and rye can use the Gluten-Free (GF) flour mix on page 6 and 156 in most recipes. It is also important to use GF vinegars, salad dressings, seasonings, bouillons and other ingredients called for in this book. For a complete list of products to use and products to avoid, see Bette Hagman's "The Gluten-Free Gourmet" and "More From The Gluten-Free Gourmet". Bette's books offer hundreds of recipes to help celiacs and others eat a wide variety of heretofore forbidden foods.

PREPARING BEANS FOR USE IN RECIPES

Cooked beans can be purchased pre-cooked in cans, or in 1-5 lb. packages from the grocery store. Dry beans can also be ordered in bulk from many co-ops and bulk food outlets. Bulk beans are usually about 1/2 the cost of pre-packaged beans. Repackage in air-tight containers.

BEAN ARITHMETIC

- A pound of beans measures about 2 cups dry, 6 cups cooked (Some varieties only double in volume).
- A pound of dry beans ground to a fine flour measures approximately 5 cups.
- Use 3 cups of water per cup of dry beans for soaking
- A pound of dry beans makes about 9 servings of baked beans, 12 servings of bean soup.
- A one-pound can of cooked beans measures about 1 2/3 cups.

"The Michigan Bean Cookbook," published by the Michigan Bean Commission

SOAKING DRY BEANS

Dry beans, whole peas, and split peas (unless used in soup) need soaking before cooking. Lentils do not.

- Overnight soak: Wash and sort beans; place in large sauce pan with 6 cups of water per pound of beans. Let stand overnight.
- Quick soak: Follow above instructions, but bring beans and water to a boil and cook 2 minutes. Remove from heat, cover, and let stand 1 hour.
- Cracked bean Quick soak: To 2 c. of beans that have been coarsely cracked using a hand grain cracker, blender, or small coffee grinder, add 4 cups boiling water. Cover and let stand 5 minutes, rinse (in strainer) and drain.

Whole, soaked beans can be cooked in a variety of ways, or frozen to speed cooking time even further. Cook soaked beans slowly over low heat to prevent broken or floating skins. A tablespoon of oil or butter added during cooking reduces foaming and boil-overs.

COOKING TIMES

These times are approximate. They differ according to altitude, age and moisture content of beans, *and* soaking method. The following list is a fairly complete list of average cooking times for soaked beans:

Black beans - 1 to 1 1/2 hrs.
Black-eyed peas - 1 to 1 1/2 hr.
Garbanzo beans - 2 to 2 1/2 hr.
Great Northern beans - 1 to 1 1/2 hrs.
Kidney beans - 1 1/2 to 2 hrs.
Lentils - 30-45 min. (NO soaking required.)
Limas, baby - 1 to 1 1/2 hrs.
Pink, pinto and red beans - 1 1/2 to 2 hrs.
Soybeans - 3 to 3 1/2 hrs.
Split peas, green and yellow - 35 to 45 min. (NO soaking required.)
White beans (navy) small - 1 to 1 1/2 hr.

Note: *Old beans ground to a flour still cook in only 3 minutes for soups. If using very old beans, make a small amount of soup to test for bitter flavor before using in soups or breads, etc.*

COOKING CRACKED BEANS

Place soaked cracked beans in saucepan with hot water to cover. Bring to a boil; cover pan, then turn heat to medium-low and cook for 15-25 minutes, depending on texture desired (firm for stir fry or to mix with cracked wheat or pilaf, soft for creamy soups, casseroles or loaves).

- Cracked soaked beans are excellent to add to stir fry. Cook in a small amount of oil until lightly browned.
- Add soaked, drained cracked beans to soups and cook for 20-30 minutes.
- Mix soaked, drained cracked beans with equal parts rice and cook for pilaf.
- Use slightly firm cooked cracked beans as a hamburger substitute or mix 1/2 cracked beans and 1/2 hamburger.

COOKING LENTILS

To cook lentils, combine 2 c. lentils and 5 c. water in a saucepan. Bring to boiling, reduce heat, cover tightly, and boil gently for 30 minutes. Lentils do not require pre-soaking. Cook sprouted lentils only 5-10 min.

COOKING BEAN "FLOUR"

No more soaking, boiling, simmering or waiting for cooked beans!

Soups, Sauces, Gravies, Thickeners Beans ground to a fine flour can be mixed with cold water and then whisked into seasoned water to make an *almost instant soup or thickener* in only 3 minutes... (learn how in the Hearty Bean Soups Section), refried beans in only 5 minutes for bean-filled burritos in a flash!

To cook bean, pea or lentil flour soups in a microwave, whisk flour into cool, seasoned water in a large microwavable bowl. Cook at full power for 1 minute, or until mixture boils. Stir well, then cook an additional 2 minutes.

See page 155 to make "Instant Mashed Beans" which can be used in any recipe calling for cooked mashed beans, including sandwich fillings and dips.

Bean flour combined with wheat flour accomplishes protein complimentation. This timesaving method is an excellent way to increase the protein in your meals and to introduce beans a little at a time. Bean flour can be used in any recipe calling for flour by *replacing up to 25% of the wheat flour with any variety of bean flour.*

I most often use baby lima or small white beans because they are the mildest in flavor and lightest in color. If the recipe calls for 2 c. wheat flour, you could add up to 1/2 c. bean flour and 1 1/2 c. wheat flour.

COOKING IN A CROCK POT

Place washed and sorted beans in boiling water (enough to cover) and simmer for 10 minutes. Drain off water. Then place beans in crockery cooker and add 6 cups of water per pound of beans and seasonings to taste. Cook on low 12 hrs.

COOKING IN A PRESSURE COOKER

Soak washed and sorted beans by either the overnight or quick method. Drain and rinse. Place in pressure cooker; cooker should be no more than 1/3 filled to allow for expansion of beans. Add water to cover and 1 T. of oil to reduce foaming.

Cover; cook at 10 pounds pressure 10-20 minutes, depending on size of bean. **OR**, place washed and sorted beans - unsoaked - in pressure cooker with 3 times as much water as beans and 2-3 teaspoons of oil or butter. Cover; cook at 15 pounds pressure for 30 minutes for small beans, 40 minutes for large beans. Variance in time is due to the inherent texture of each different variety of bean.

Some soften more quickly than others. Lentils and split peas cook quickly using conventional methods, so do *not* need to be pressure cooked.

See **HOME CANNING** section to pressure bottle beans (the fastest, most economical way to use beans). These beans can be kept at room temperature and used like commercially canned beans.

COOKING IN A MICROWAVE

Wash and sort a pound of dry beans. Place beans and 8 cups of water in 5 quart casserole, along with any seasonings called for in the recipe. Microwave at full power 8-10 minutes or until boiling. Cover with plastic wrap and/or casserole lid. Let stand 1 hour.

Stir several times and add hot water as needed to keep beans covered as they absorb the soaking water. Cook at full power again 20 minutes; reduce power level to 50% and cook another 30-40 minutes or until tender.

Beans may also be soaked using the overnight or quick method, then cooked at full power for 8-10 minutes or until boiling, then at 50% power 20-40 minutes or until tender.

Note: Boilovers are common using the microwave and I have not found that this method saves any cooking time.

COOKING TIPS

- If a recipe calls for lemon juice, vinegar or tomatoes, wait until the beans are almost tender before adding them, as the acid in these items slows the softening process (unless using a pressure cooker).

- At high altitudes or in hard water areas, increase both the soaking time and cooking time, as necessary.

- Gently simmer beans to prevent them from bursting, causing floating skins which must then be skimmed off of soups or stews.

- Two to three teaspoons of oil or butter added during cooking reduces foaming and boil-overs.

STORING COOKED BEANS

- Freeze cooked beans (whole or cracked) in 1-2 cup portions in zip-loc bags. Flatten bag, squeezing out air, then seal and lay flat in freezer. I often freeze quite a few bags at a time, so I lay them in a stack 6-8" tall. Beans will keep 3-6 months. Add frozen to any recipe that will be cooked, as in soups, stews, casseroles, loaves and breads, or thaw to use in salads and dips.
- Store cooked beans in a covered container for 3-5 days in the refrigerator. Beans spoil easily, so be careful not to keep them too long.
- Dry beans can be bottled, using a pressure canner, and have a shelf life of at least 1 year. See bottling information on page 158.

BEAN COMBINATIONS

Commercial Bean Soup Mixes have become more popular in the last few years, and can be made at home, using the following quantities, or simply use any beans that are readily available in your area. The variety of beans helps add color as well as flavor. Mix and store for future use (or cook and freeze), to quickly and easily be able to make attractive, nutritious bean dishes. A jar of layered beans (as described below) makes a great present.

3-Bean Mix (makes 1 quart) - 1 cup kidney, 1 1/2 c. navy or small white, 1 1/2 c. pinto

5-Bean Mix (makes 2 quarts) - 2 cups each pinto, navy or small white, garbanzo, 1 cup each kidney, black

10-Bean Mix (makes 3 quarts) - 1 cup each navy or small white, soybean or mung, lima, lentil, garbanzo, kidney, black, pea (whole or split), 2 cups each cranberry or pink and pinto

13-Bean and Grain Mix (makes 6 quarts) - 1 cup each wheat, yellow peas, lima, mung, garbanzo, 2 cups each navy or small white, blackeye, green peas, lentil, black, and 3 cups each pinto, barley and kidney.

For a **Gift of a Healthy Heart**, place the following in a heart-shaped basket: 2 c. Bean Flour in a calico bag or circle of fabric; Jar with layered beans; Recipes for using Bean Flour or a copy of COUNTRY BEANS. Great for healthy OR sick friends, new neighbors, old neighbors, weddings, funerals, or just to show how much you care.

EQUIPMENT AND SUPPLIES

BOB'S RED MILL NATURAL FOODS, Milwaukie, OR 97222. 1-800-349-2173, www.bobsredmill.com. Bean, pea and lentil flours, whole grains and whole grain products, books and equipment. Call or write for mail-order catalog or supplier.

EMERGENCY ESSENTIALS, Orem, UT. 1-800-999-1863, www.beprepared.com. 72-hour kits; camping, emergency and storage supplies, equipment, containers; preparedness books and videos, foods, water purifiers, tents, backpack foods.

K-TEC, Orem, UT. 1-800-748-5400, www.k-tecusa.com, manufacturer of the Champ Blender, K-TEC Kitchen Mill, and Kitchenetics Kitchen Machine (with heavy duty blender). The Kitchen Mill is guaranteed to grind all beans and grains.

LIFE SPROUTS, Hyrum, UT. 1-800-241-1516, www.lifesprouts.com. An excellent source for sprouters, sprouting seeds and storage containers. Their seed mixes are specially combined to provide complete nutrition.

LM PUBLICATIONS, 1-888-554-3727, www.learta.com. Books, Videos and More. The Amazing Wheat Book, Living with Basics CD, The Herb Walk Video and DVD, Plant ID Game Cards, and Nature's Medicine Chest Plant ID Cards.

NATURAL HEALTH SOLUTIONS, 1-877-359-1221, www.BetterHealth-Online.com. Nutrition Counseling with Whole Foods ..for Better Health - the *Natural* Way. If you're not getting your 9-13 servings of raw fruits and vegetables every day, there's ***Juice* Plus+** ...17 colorful fruits and veggies in Capsule, Gummie or Chewable form . ***Juice* Plus+** is also your best choice for compact, *nutritious* Food Storage. Visit our websites, www.JuicePlusforPrevention.com, and www.ScienceandHealthNews.com, to obtain product information and our published, peer-reviewed research. OR call our Information Hotline 24 hours a day at 1-800-624-7671.

NATURAL MEALS PUBLISHING, 1-888-232-6706 , www.naturalmeals.com. Quick Wholesome Foods Video and DVD, Cookbooks, Better Health Handbook, Common-sense Preparedness Guide, NutriBiotic GSE (for water purification - protection from giardia and other waterborne pathogens; protection from colds and flu; disinfecting, and first aid).

WALTON FEED, INC, 1-800-847-0465. P. O. Box 307, Montpelier, ID 83254, www.waltonfeed.com. Beans, grains, equipment, books, videos, containers, dehydrated foods, seeds, 72-hour kits. Hand and electric grain mills to crack or grind grains and beans .

Alphabetical Index To Recipes

All Purpose Seasoning (GF) 65
Allergies to Beans and Wheat 180
Alphabet Soup Mix 99
Apple-Bean Cookies (GF) 137
Apple-Cinnamon Snax (GF) 133
Asparagus Noodle Soup 96
Asparagus—Tomato Stir Fry (GF) 130
Avocado Bean Salad (GF) 44
Baked Scones 23
Banana Nut Bread 22
Banana Orange Bars (GF) 136
Barley Lima Soup 97
Bean 'N Rice Burgers 69
Bean and Barley Stew 84
Bean and Mushroom Soup (GF) 91
Bean and Nut Bread 21
Bean and Pepper Stir Fry (GF) 116
Bean and Rice Burritos 108
Bean Combinations 180
Bean Sprout 'n Rice Salad (GF) 38
Beanamole (GF) 53
Beanchiladas 106
Beans 'n Rice Salad (GF) 42
Beans and Barley Soup 85
Beany Tuna Delight (GF) 57
Best Creamy Corn Chowder (GF) 86
Better Breakfasts 7
Black Bean and Tomato Soup(GF) 88
Black Bean Burritos 106
Black Bean Soup (GF) 88
Black Bean Soup and Salad (GF) 95
Black Bean Taco Pizza 106
Blender Mayonnaise (GF) 31
Bob's Best Biscuits (GF) 21
Bottled Beans (GF) 158
Breads 12, 18, 24
Breakfast Pita Pizzas 9
Broiled Bean and Tuna Sandwiches (GF) 54
Brown Gravy (GF) 61
Brown Rice Burgers 69
Burritos Con Queso 110
Buttermilk Biscuits (GF) 21
Buying Beans 173
Carob and Soy Brownies (GF) 138
Carob Chip Mint Cookies (GF) 142
Carob Crackle (GF) 150
Carob Cream Pie (GF) 145
Carob Fruit Squares (GF) 137
Casseroles and One-Dish Meals 100
Cheese 'n Onion Bread 28
Cheese Patties (GF) 67
Cheese Sauce (GF) 60
Cheesey Bean Dip (GF) 52
Cheesey Beans in Crepes (GF) 128
Cheesey Sandwiches (GF) 54
Chicken and Broccoli Quiche (GF) 126
Chili Rice Salad (GF) 36
Chili-Noodle Dish 118
Chinese Garbanzo Bean Salad (GF) 42
Cinnamon-Apple Muffins 17
Clair's Oriental Rice Soup 94
Clam 'n Bean Soup (GF) 160
Clam and Bean Chowder (GF) 90
Clamless Chowder (GF) 91
Coconut-Oatmeal Cake 145
Colorful Bean Bake (GF) 109
Company Dinners 124
Company Salad Bar (GF) 48
Converting Recipes to Gluten-Free 177
Cooked Cracked or Mashed Beans 155
Cooking Bean Flour 3, 79, 173, 180

Cooking Options....154
Corn and Carrot Soup (GF)....82
Corn Dodgers (GF)....19
Country Blend Seasonings....64
Country Vegetable Soup (GF)....160
Cranberry Orange Breakfast Squares....14
Cream of Asparagus Soup (GF)....90
Cream of Chicken Soup Substitute (GF).80
Cream of Spinach Soup (GF)....86
Creamy "Pumpkin" Pie (GF)....144
Creamy 4-Vegetable Casserole (GF)....104
Creamy Avocado Sandwich (GF)....55
Creamy Banana-Berry Drink (GF)....11
Creamy Broccoli Soup (GF)....93
Creamy Cabbage Soup (GF)....92
Creamy Chicken Double Bean Casserole (GF)....103
Creamy Dressing (GF)....32
Creamy Hot Bean Salad (GF)....46
Creamy Lima Lentil (GF)....83
Creamy Potato Bisque (GF)....85
Creamy Soy Soup (GF)....97
Creamy Tomato Basil Soup (GF)....85
Creamy Tuna Salad (GF)....38
Creamy Vegetable Bean Dish (GF)....112
Creamy Yellow Pea (GF)....83
Crepes with Hot "Crab" Filling (GF)....129
Cruciferous Soup (GF)....163
Crunchy Baby Lima and Cheddar Slaw (GF)....40
Crusty Mini-Wheats....29
Cucumber Dressing (GF)....32
Cucumber Salad (GF)....45
Desserts....134
Dieter's Delight (GF)....36
Dips & Sandwich Fillings....51
Double Cheesy Tacos or Tortillas (GF)..105
Dressings, Sauces, Toppings....30
Easy Bean Dip (GF)....56
Easy Layered Spinach Salad (GF)....49
Easy Thousand Island (GF)....32
Egg Foo Yong (GF)....70
Emma's Brown and Serve Rolls....25
Fantastic Instant Corn Chowder (GF)....85
Favorite Buttermilk Dressing (GF)....31
Fiesta Soup (GF)....96
Flavored Sesame Oil....156
Freezer Bean Burritos....106
Fresh Garden Salad (GF)....40
Fresh Spinach Sandwich (GF)....54
Fresh Vegetable Soup (GF)....93
Fresh Zucchini Salad (GF)....46
Frozen Cooked Beans Or Rice....156
Garbanzo Bean and Tofu Salad (GF)....35
Garbanzo Bean Salad (GF)....41
Garbanzo Bean Sandwich Spread (GF)...55
Garbanzo Patties (GF)....69
Garbanzo-Wheat or Rice Patties (GF)....68
Gingerbread Bars (GF)....142
Gluten-Free Info....6, 156, 166, 167, 180
Golden Grains Brown Bread....28
Grandma's Best Date Nut Pudding (GF)....144
Grandpa's Carrot Cake (GF)....146
Great Chili Soup (GF)....161
Great Wheat Chips....132
Great Wheat Muffins....16
Green Bean and Olive Salad (GF)....45
Green Rice Pilaf (GF)....121
Guacamole (GF)....53
Harvest Special (GF)....89
Harvest Special (GF)....163
Hearty Bean Soups....80
Hearty Oatmeal Bread....27
Hearty Pinto Bean Soup (GF)....84
Hearty Red Beans and Rice Soup (GF)....98

Hearty Rice Soup (GF) 94
Herb Dumplings (GF) 82
Hi-Pro Cereal Mix....9
High Protein Applejacks....14
High Protein Crumbly Topping (GF)....63
Home Canning....157
Honey Cookies (GF)....137
Honey Graham Crackers....141
Honey Raisin Cookies (GF)....140
Hot and Sour Soup (GF)....87
Hot and Spicy Black Beans
and Rice (GF)....111
Hot Pepper Bean Soup (GF)....96
Hot Red Bean Soup (GF)....158
How to Grind Dry Beans to a Flour....174
Indonesian Black Beans and
Fried Rice (GF)....116
Information Section....164
Instant Mashed Beans....155
Instant Pea Soup (GF)....81
Instant Refried Bean Mix (GF)....123
Italian "Meat" Balls for Spaghetti....72
Italian Mini Loaves....77
Italian Mini-Tofu Loaves....130
Japanese Red Rice (GF)....114
Layered Bean & Rice Burrito Casserole 108
Lemon Pepper (GF)....67
Lemon Sauce (GF)....144
Lentil Garbanzo Patties....69
Lentil Salad (GF)....37
Lentil Soup (GF)....86
Lentil Soup Seasoning (GF)....66
Lentil Vegetable Soup (GF)....92
Lentil-Garbanzo Casserole (GF)....103
Lima Bean Salad (GF)....49
Linguine With Crab Sauce....127
Little Lima Bean & Chiles
Casseroles (GF)....111
Lizzy's Easy Enchiladas....107
Lizzy's Oriental Salad....39
Lo-Mein....102
Macaroni Soup....89
Magic Crust Taco Pie (GF)....105
Mama's Magic Muffin Mix....13
Mandarin Tangerine Freeze....11
Manhattan "Clam" Chowder (GF)....161
Many Bean Soup (GF)....88
Marinated Bean Salad (GF)....38
Mediterranean Salad (GF)....39
Mexi-Pita Bar....34
Mexican Bean Bake (GF)....101
Mexican Bean Gravy (GF)....61
Mexican Bean Puffs....75
Mexican Bean Quiche (GF)....126
Mexican Dinner In A Pita....37
Mexican Fiesta Blend Vegetables (GF)..121
Mexican Hot Pockets (GF)....52
Mexican Mini Loaves (GF)....129
Mexican Pilaf (GF)....120
Millet and Bean Casserole (GF)....109
Million $$ Bars (Super Rich!) (GF)....138
Minestrone Soup (GF)....84
Mini Casseroles (GF)....113
Mini Oaties....27
Mini-Mock Salmon Loaves....77
Minty SunnySeed Squares (GF)....150
Moist Muffins....13
Moist Nut 'n Honey Granola....8
Mung Sprout Salad (GF)....46
Mushroom Barley Soup....94
Mushrooms, Beans and Rice (GF)....112
New England "Clam" Chowder (GF)...161

No-Wheat Date Cookies (GF) 135
Noodle-Bean Soup 93
Nut 'n Honey Bran Muffins 15
Nutty Banana Bread 13
Nutty Gingerbread (GF) 147
Oatmeal Date and Nut Bread 22
Okara Orange Crunch (GF) 150
One and One-Half Bean Salad (GF) 39
Onion Dip 53
Onion Flavored Topping (GF) 63
Oriental "Meat" Balls 72
Oriental Beans and Rice Quiche (GF) 127
Oriental Blend Vegetables (GF) 121
Oriental Cashew Pasta Salad (GF) 43
Oriental Dressing (GF) 32
Oriental Omelettes (GF) 122
Oriental Pilaf (GF) 120
Oriental Rice Soup (GF) 98
Oriental Sauce (GF) 59
Oriental Spinach Quiche (GF) 127
Oriental Stir Fry (GF) 110
Oriental Vegetable Soup (GF) 95
Oriental Vegetables Almondine (GF) 102
Overnight Bean Salad (GF) 41
Patties and Loaves 68, 74
Peanut Butter Banana Bars (GF) 140
Peanut Butter Mounds (GF) 141
Perfect Buttermilk Pancakes (GF) 15
Perfect Buttermilk Pancakes (GF) 15
Perfect Pancakes (GF) 15
Perfect Pancakes (GF) 15
Petite Peas and Bean Salad (GF) 45
Picnic Salad (GF) 34
Pinto Bean Bread 26
Pinto Bean-Apple Cake (GF) 146
Popcorn Seasoning (GF) 67
Potato Bean Soup (GF) 162
Powdered Sucanat 156
Pretty As A Present Soup 99
Quick and Easy Corn Bread Squares 20
Quick Red Lentil Soup (GF) 83
Quick Skillet Quiche (GF) 103
Quick Tofu Burger Mix 72
Raisin-Nut Pinto Bean Cake (GF) 148
Raspberry Freeze (GF) 11
Raspberry Oat Bars 135
Red and White Broiled
Sandwiches (GF) 56
Red and White Pasta Salad 35
Red and White Potato Soup (GF) 91
Red and Yellow Dinner (GF) 116
Red Bean Salad (GF) 47
Red Lentil Soup (GF) 98
Red Pepper Salad (GF) 41
Refried Beans (GF) 123
Refried Beans, FAST (GF) 123
Ribbon Cookies (GF) 142
Rice and Bean Salad (GF) 50
Rich Oatmeal Butterscotch
Chip Cookies 139
Rita's Lentil Soup (GF) 82
Ruth's Honey Sponge Cake (GF) 147
Salads 33
Salsa Verde (GF) 60
Salt-Free Mexican (Mild) (GF) 65
Savory Bean Stew (GF) 95
Sesame, Bean and Corn Bread 19
Sesame-Ginger Snax (GF) 133
Sheepherder's Hearty Soup (GF) 89
Side Dishes 119
Snacks 131
Southern Red Beans and Rice (GF) 115
Soy Mayonnaise (GF) 31
Soy Milk (GF) 97, 152
Soybean Lasagne (GF) 101
Soybean Tuna Salad (GF) 50

Soyburgers 71
Spanish Bean Loaf 76
Spanish Rice and Beans (GF) 117
Spanish Rice Salad (GF) 43
Speedy Gonzales Bean and
Cucumber Salad (GF) 44
Speedy Mexi-Bean Salad (GF) 47
Spelt Bread (for the Bread Machine) 26
Spicy Apple Cookies 139
Spicy Black Bean Taco Salad (GF) 48
Spicy Buttermilk Ranch (GF) 31
Spicy Continental Seasoning (GF) 67
Spicy Cucumber Dip (GF) 56
Spicy Honey Nuts 8
Spicy Lentil Soup (GF) 87
Spicy Oatmeal Muffins 17
Spicy Pinto Cupcakes (GF) 148
Spicy Red Sauce (GF) 60
Spicy Spanish Gravy (GF) 76
Spinach Loaves (GF) 113
Split Pea Soup (GF) 159
Spotted Turtle Bread 29
Sprouted Lentil Soup (GF) 92
Stupendous Bean Patties 69
Sukiyaki Supreme (GF) 118
Sunchoke Salad (GF) 44
Super Corn Chips (GF) 132
Super Protein Patties 68
Surprisingly Yummy Spicy
Lentil Stew (GF) 92
Sweet and Sour Lentil Salad (GF) 49
Sweet and Sour Sauce (GF) 59
Sweet and Sour Veggies (GF) 114
Taco Snax (GF) 133
Tamale Pie (GF) 115
Tamale Pie Gravy (GF) 61
Tamale Soup (GF) 97
Tangy Pasta and Beans (GF) 37
Tapioca Bread (GF) 25
Tender Zucchini Bread 23
The Muffin Bar 16
Three-Minute Cream of
Chicken Soup (GF) 80
Toasty Beaners (GF) 55
Tofu (GF) 152, 153
Tofu and Okara 151, 152, 153
Tofu Curry Salad (GF) 50
Tofu Eggnog (GF) 11
Tofu Pepper Stir Fry (GF) 108
Tofu-Sesame Bread Sticks 20
Tomato Basil Sprout Soup (GF) 98
Tomato Bean Soup (GF) 90
Tomato Vegetable Soup (GF) 159
Tomato-Basil Sauce (GF) 60
Tomato-Bean Filling or Salad (GF) 57
Triple Duty GF Muffin Mix (GF) 13
Tuna-Bean Sandwich Filling (GF) 52
2-Bean Skillet Supper (GF) 104
Vegetable Bean Quiche (GF) 125
Vegetable Bean Salad (GF) 47
Vegetable Bean Soup (GF) 159
Vegetable Mushroom (GF) 163
Vegetable Pasta Sauce (GF) 59
Vegetable Seasoning (GF) 66
Versatile Bean Mini-Loaves 75
Wheat Curry Salad 36
Where to Buy Publications,
Equipment and Supplies 183, 184
White Bean Gravy (GF) 61
White Bean Spread 57
Whole Meal Layered Salad (GF) 35
Whole Wheat Pinto Bean Bread 26
Zucchini Quiche (GF) 126

Index to Recipes by Section

BETTER BREAKFASTS 7
Breakfast Pita Pizzas.......9
Creamy Banana-Berry Drink (GF).......11
Hi-Pro Cereal Mix.......9
Mandarin Tangerine Freeze.......11
Moist Nut 'n Honey Granola.......8
Perfect Buttermilk Pancakes (GF).......15
Perfect Pancakes (GF).......15
Raspberry Freeze (GF).......11
Spicy Honey Nuts.......8
Tofu Eggnog (GF).......11

BREADS 12, 18, 24
Baked Scones.......23
Banana Nut Bread.......22
Bean and Nut Bread.......21
Bob's Best Biscuits (GF).......21
Buttermilk Biscuits (GF).......21
Cheese 'n Onion Bread.......28
Cinnamon-Apple Muffins.......17
Corn Dodgers (GF).......19
Cranberry Orange Breakfast Squares.......14
Crusty Mini-Wheats.......29
Emma's Brown and Serve Rolls.......25
Golden Grains Brown Bread.......28
Great Wheat Muffins.......16
Hearty Oatmeal Bread.......27
High Protein Applejacks.......14
Mama's Magic Muffin Mix.......13
Mini Oaties.......27
Moist Muffins.......13
Nut 'n Honey Bran Muffins.......15
Nutty Banana Bread.......13
Oatmeal Date and Nut Bread.......22
Perfect Buttermilk Pancakes (GF).......15
Perfect Pancakes (GF).......15
Pinto Bean Bread.......26
Quick and Easy Corn Bread Squares.......20
Sesame, bean and Corn bread.......19
Spelt Bread (for the Bread Machine).......26
Spicy Oatmeal Muffins.......17
Spotted Turtle Bread.......29
Tapioca Bread (GF).......25
Tender Zucchini Bread.......23
The Muffin Bar.......16
Tofu-Sesame Bread Sticks.......20
Triple Duty GF Muffin Mix (GF).......13
Whole Wheat Pinto Bean Bread.......26

SALADS 33
Avocado Bean Salad (GF).......44
Bean Sprout 'n Rice Salad (GF).......38
Beans 'n Rice Salad (GF).......42
Chili Rice Salad (GF).......36
Chinese Garbanzo Bean Salad (GF).......42
Company Salad Bar (GF).......48
Creamy Hot Bean Salad (GF).......46
Creamy Tuna Salad (GF).......38
Crunchy Baby Lima and Cheddar Slaw (GF).......40
Cucumber Salad (GF).......45
Dieter's Delight (GF).......36
Easy Layered Spinach Salad (GF).......49
Fresh Garden Salad (GF).......40
Fresh Zucchini Salad (GF).......46
Garbanzo Bean and Tofu Salad (GF).......35
Garbanzo Bean Salad (GF).......41
Green Bean and Olive Salad (GF).......45
Lentil Salad (GF).......37
Lima Bean Salad (GF).......49
Lizzy's Oriental Salad.......39
Marinated Bean Salad (GF).......38
Mediterranean Salad (GF).......39
Mexi-Pita Bar.......34
Mexican Dinner In A Pita.......37
Mung Sprout Salad (GF).......46
One and One-Half Bean Salad (GF).......39
Oriental Cashew Pasta Salad (GF).......43
Overnight Bean Salad (GF).......41
Petite Peas and Bean Salad (GF).......45
Picnic Salad (GF).......34
Red and White Pasta Salad.......35
Red Bean Salad (GF).......47
Red Pepper Salad (GF).......41
Rice and Bean Salad (GF).......50
Soybean Tuna Salad (GF).......50
Spanish Rice Salad (GF).......43
Speedy Gonzales Bean and Cucumber Salad (GF).......44
Speedy Mexi-Bean Salad (GF).......47
Spicy Black Bean Taco Salad (GF).......48
Sunchoke Salad (GF).......44
Sweet and Sour Lentil Salad (GF).......49
Tangy Pasta and Beans (GF).......37

(GF) - Gluten-Free

Tofu Curry Salad (GF)..50
Vegetable Bean Salad (GF) 47
Wheat Curry Salad ....36Whole Meal Layered Salad (GF)...35

DRESSINGS, SAUCES, TOPPINGS 30
Blender Mayonnaise (GF).................................31
Brown Gravy (GF) 61
Cheese Sauce (GF)...128
Creamy Dressing (GF)..32
Cucumber Dressing (GF)...................................32
Easy Thousand Island (GF) 32
Favorite Buttermilk Dressing (GF) 31
High Protein Crumbly Topping (GF) 63
Lemon Sauce (GF)..144
Mexican Bean Gravy (GF)..................................61
Onion Flavored Topping (GF) 63
Oriental Dressing (GF) 32
Oriental Sauce (GF)..59
Salsa Verde (GF)..60
Soy Mayonnaise (GF) 31
Spicy Buttermilk Ranch (GF).............................31
Spicy Red Sauce (GF) 60
Spicy Spanish Gravy (GF)..................................76
Sweet and Sour Sauce (GF)................................59
Tamale Pie Gravy (GF).......................................61
Tomato-Basil Sauce (GF)....................................60
Vegetable Pasta Sauce (GF) 59
White Bean Gravy (GF)......................................61

DIPS & SANDWICH FILLINGS 51
Beanamole (GF)...53
Beany Tuna Delight (GF) 57
Broiled Bean and Tuna Sandwiches (GF).........54
Cheesey Bean Dip (GF) 52
Cheesey Sandwiches (GF) 54
Creamy Avocado Sandwich (GF).....................55
Easy Bean Dip (GF)..56
Fresh Spinach Sandwich (GF) 54
Garbanzo Bean Sandwich Spread (GF) 55
Guacamole (GF) 53
Mexican Hot Pockets (GF) 52
Onion Dip...53
Red and White Broiled Sandwiches (GF).........56
Spicy Cucumber Dip (GF) 56
Toasty Beaners (GF)...55
Tomato-Bean Filling or Salad (GF)...................57
Tuna-Bean Sandwich Filling (GF) 52
White Bean Spread 57

COUNTRY BLEND SEASONINGS 64
All Purpose Seasoning (GF) 65
Lemon Pepper (GF) 67
Lentil Soup Seasoning (GF)...............................66
Popcorn Seasoning (GF)....................................67
Salt-Free Mexican (Mild) (GF)..........................65
Spicy Continental Seasoning (GF)....................67
Vegetable Seasoning (GF).................................66

PATTIES AND LOAVES 68, 74
Bean 'N Rice Burgers...69
Brown Rice Burgers 69
Cheese Patties (GF) 69
Egg Foo Yong (GF)...70
Garbanzo Patties (GF) 71
Garbanzo-Wheat or Rice Patties (GF) 70
Italian "Meat" Balls for Spaghetti......................73
Italian Mini Loaves 76
Lentil Garbanzo Patties......................................71
Mexican Bean Puffs 75
Mexican Mini Loaves 77
Mini-Mock Salmon Loaves...............................77
Oriental "Meat" Balls 73
Quick Tofu Burger Mix 73
Soyburgers 72
Spanish Bean Loaf..76
Stupendous Bean Patties...................................71
Super Protein Patties 70
Taco Soybean Patties 72
Versatile Bean Mini-Loaves...............................75

HEARTY BEAN SOUPS 78
Alphabet Soup Mix..99
Asparagus Noodle Soup...................................96
Barley Lima Soup 97
Beans and Barley Soup 85
Bean and Barley Stew 84
Bean and Mushroom Soup (GF) 91
Best Creamy Corn Chowder (GF) 86
Black Bean and Tomato Soup(GF)....................88
Black Bean Soup (GF) 88
Black Bean Soup and Salad (GF).......................95
Clair's Oriental Rice Soup..................................94
Clam and Bean Chowder (GF)..........................90
Clamless Chowder (GF).....................................91
Corn and Carrot Soup (GF) 82
Cream of Asparagus Soup (GF)........................90
Cream of Chicken Soup Substitute (GF)...........80
Cream of Spinach Soup (GF).............................86

Creamy Broccoli Soup (GF) ... 93
Creamy Cabbage Soup (GF) ... 92
Creamy Lima Lentil (GF) ... 83
Creamy Potato Bisque (GF) ... 85
Creamy Soy Soup (GF) ... 97
Creamy Tomato Basil Soup (GF) ... 85
Creamy Yellow Pea (GF) ... 83
Fantastic Instant Corn Chowder (GF) ... 85
Fiesta Soup (GF) ... 96
Fresh Vegetable Soup (GF) ... 93
Harvest Special (GF) ... 89
Hearty Pinto Bean Soup (GF) ... 84
Hearty Red Beans and Rice Soup (GF) ... 98
Hearty Rice Soup (GF) ... 94
Herb Dumplings (GF) ... 82
Hot and Sour Soup (GF) ... 87
Hot Pepper Bean Soup (GF) ... 96
"Instant Pea Soup" (GF) ... 81
Lentil Soup (GF) ... 86
Lentil Vegetable Soup (GF) ... 92
Macaroni Soup ... 89
Many Bean Soup (GF) ... 88
Minestrone Soup (GF) ... 84
Mushroom Barley Soup ... 94
Noodle-Bean Soup ... 93
Oriental Rice Soup (GF) ... 98
Oriental Vegetable Soup (GF) ... 95
Pretty As A Present Soup ... 99
Quick Red Lentil (GF) ... 83
Red and White Potato Soup (GF) ... 91
Red Lentil Soup (GF) ... 98
Rita's Lentil Soup (GF) ... 82
Savory Bean Stew (GF) ... 95
Sheepherder's Hearty Soup (GF) ... 89
Spicy Lentil Soup (GF) ... 87
Sprouted Lentil Soup (GF) ... 92
Surprisingly Yummy Spicy Lentil Stew (GF) ... 92
Tamale Soup (GF) ... 97
Three-Minute Cream of Chicken Soup (GF) ... 80
Tomato Basil Sprout Soup (GF) ... 98
Tomato Bean Soup (GF) ... 90

CASSEROLES AND ONE-DISH MEALS ... 100
2-Bean Skillet Supper (GF) ... 104
Bean and Pepper Stir Fry (GF) ... 116
Bean and Rice Burritos ... 108
Beanchiladas ... 106
Black Bean Burritos ... 106
Black Bean Taco Pizza ... 106
Burritos Con Queso ... 110
Chili-Noodle Dish ... 118
Colorful Bean Bake (GF) ... 109
Creamy 4-Vegetable Casserole (GF) ... 104
Creamy Chicken Double Bean Casserole (GF) ... 103
Creamy Vegetable Bean Dish (GF) ... 112
Double Cheesy Tacos or Tortillas (GF) ... 105
Freezer Bean Burritos ... 106
Hot and Spicy Black Beans and Rice (GF) ... 111
Indonesian Black Beans and Fried Rice (GF) ... 116
Japanese Red Rice (GF) ... 114
Layered Bean & Rice Burrito Casserole ... 108
Lentil-Garbanzo Casserole (GF) ... 103
Little Lima Bean & Chiles Casseroles (GF) ... 111
Lizzy's Easy Enchiladas ... 107
Lo-Mein ... 102
Magic Crust Taco Pie (GF) ... 105
Mexican Bean Bake (GF) ... 101
Millet and Bean Casserole (GF) ... 109
Mini Casseroles (GF) ... 113
Mushrooms, Beans and Rice (GF) ... 112
Oriental Stir Fry (GF) ... 110
Oriental Vegetables Almondine (GF) ... 102
Quick Skillet Quiche (GF) ... 103
Red and Yellow Dinner (GF) ... 116
Southern Red Beans and Rice (GF) ... 115
Soybean Lasagne (GF) ... 101
Spanish Rice and Beans (GF) ... 117
Spinach Loaves (GF) ... 113
Sukiyaki Supreme (GF) ... 118
Sweet and Sour Veggies (GF) ... 114
Tamale Pie (GF) ... 115
Tofu Pepper Stir Fry (GF) ... 108

SIDE DISHES ... 119
FAST Refried Beans (GF) ... 123
Green Rice Pilaf (GF) ... 121
Instant Refried Bean Mix (GF) ... 123
Mexican Fiesta Blend Vegetables (GF) ... 121
Mexican Pilaf (GF) ... 120
Oriental Blend Vegetables (GF) ... 121
Oriental Omelettes (GF) ... 122
Oriental Pilaf (GF) ... 120
COMPANY DINNERS ... 124

Asparagus—Tomato Stir Fry (GF) 130
Cheesey Beans in Crepes (GF) 128
Chicken and Broccoli Quiche (GF) 126
Crepes with Hot "Crab" Filling (GF) 129
Italian Mini-Tofu Loaves 130
Linguine With Crab Sauce 127
Mexican Bean Quiche (GF) 126
Mexican Mini Loaves (GF) 129
Oriental Beans and Rice Quiche (GF) 127
Oriental Spinach Quiche (GF) 127
Vegetable Bean Quiche (GF) 125
Zucchini Quiche (GF) 126

SNACKS 131
Apple-Cinnamon Snax (GF) 133
Great Wheat Chips 132
Refried Beans, *FAST* (GF) 123
Sesame-Ginger Snax (GF) 133
Super Corn Chips (GF) 132
Taco Snax (GF) 133

DESSERTS 134
Apple-Bean Cookies (GF) 137
Banana Orange Bars (GF) 136
Carob and Soy Brownies (GF) 138
Carob Chip Mint Cookies (GF) 142
Carob Crackle (GF) 150
Carob Cream Pie (GF) 145
Carob Fruit Squares (GF) 137
Coconut-Oatmeal Cake 145
Creamy "Pumpkin" Pie (GF) 144
Gingerbread Bars (GF) 142
Grandma's Best Date Nut Pudding (GF) 144
Grandpa's Carrot Cake (GF) 146
Honey Cookies (GF) 137
Honey Graham Crackers 141
Honey Raisin Cookies (GF) 140
Million $$ Bars (Super Rich!) (GF) 138
Minty SunnySeed Squares (GF) 150
No-Wheat Date Cookies (GF) 135
Nutty Gingerbread (GF) 147
Okara Orange Crunch (GF) 150
Peanut Butter Banana Bars (GF) 140
Peanut Butter Mounds (GF) 141
Pinto Bean-Apple Cake (GF) 146
Raisin-Nut Pinto Bean Cake (GF) 148
Raspberry Oat Bars 135
Ribbon Cookies (GF) 142
Rich Oatmeal Butterscotch
Chip Cookies 139
Ruth's Honey Sponge Cake (GF) 147
Spicy Apple Cookies 139
Spicy Pinto Cupcakes (GF) 148

TOFU AND OKARA 151
Soy Milk for drinking (GF) 152
Tofu (GF) 153

COOKING OPTIONS 154
Cooked Cracked or Mashed Beans 155
Flavored Sesame Oil 156
Frozen Cooked Beans Or Rice 156
Instant Mashed Beans 155
Powdered Sucanat 156

HOME CANNING 157
Bottled Beans (GF) 158
"Clam" 'n Bean Soup (GF) 160
Country Vegetable Soup (GF) 160
Cruciferous Soup (GF) 163
Great Chili Soup (GF) 161
Harvest Special (GF) 163
Hot Red Bean Soup (GF) 158
Manhattan "Clam" Chowder (GF) 161
New England "Clam" Chowder (GF) 161
Potato Bean Soup (GF) 162
Split Pea Soup (GF) 159
Tomato Vegetable Soup (GF) 159
Vegetable Bean Soup (GF) 159
Vegetable Mushroom (GF) 163

INFORMATION SECTION 164
Allergies to Wheat, etc. 177
Bean Combinations 182
Buying Beans 173
Converting Recipes to Gluten-Free 177
Cooking Bean Flour 3, 79, 173, 180
How to Grind Dry Beans to a Flour 174
Where to Buy Publications,
Equipment and Supplies 183, 184
Gluten-Free Information 6, 156, 166, 167, 180

Index To Bean Flour Recipes

BREAKFASTS
Spicy Honey Nuts 8
Moist Nut'N Honey Granola 8
Hi-Pro Cereal Mix 9

BREADS
Mama's Magic Muffin Mix 13
Triple Duty Muffin Mix 13
Cranberry Orange Breakfast Squares 14
High Protein Applejacks 14
Nut N'Honey Bran Muffins 15
Perfect Buttermilk Pancakes 15
Perfect Pancakes 15
Great Wheat Muffins 16
The Muffin Bar 16
Cinnamon-Apple Muffins 17
Sesame Corn Bread 19
Corn Dodgers 19
Quick and Easy Corn Bread Squares 20
Tofu-Sesame Bread Sticks 20
Bob's Best Biscuits 21
Oatmeal Date and Nut Bread 22
Banana Nut Bread 22
Tender Zucchini Bread 23
Baked Scones 23
Emma's Brown and Serve Rolls 25
Tapioca Bread 25
Spelt Bread (for the Bread Machine) 26
Hearty Oatmeal Bread 27
Mini Oaties 27
Cheese 'N Onion Bread 28
Crusty Mini-Wheats 28
Golden Grains Brown Bread 28

SALADS, DIPS, SAUCES, DRESSINGS
Guacamole 53
Spicy Cucumber Dip 56
Sweet and Sour Sauce 59
Vegetable Pasta Sauce 59
Tomato Basil Sauce 60
Spicy Red Sauce 59
Salsa Verde 60
Mexican Bean Gravy 61
White Bean Gravy 61
Tamale Pie Gravy 61
Cheese Sauce 128

PATTIES AND LOAVES
Super Protein Patties 68
Quick Tofu Burger Mix 72

SOUPS
Cream of Chicken Soup Substitute 80
3-Minute Cream of Chicken Soup 80
Fantastic Instant Corn Chowder 85
Corn and Carrot Soup 82
Rita's Lentil Soup 82
Creamy Lima Lentil Soup 83
Creamy Yellow Pea Soup 83
Quick Red Lentil Soup 83
Creamy Potato Bisque 85
Instant Pea Soup 81
Hot and Sour Soup 87
Spicy Lentil Soup 87
Lentil Soup 86
Sheepherder's Hearty Soup 89
Cream of Asparagus Soup 90
Red and White Potato Soup 91

Clamless Chowder....91
Creamy Cabbage Soup....92
Sprouted Lentil Soup....92
Creamy Broccoli Soup....93
Clair's Oriental Rice Soup....94
Creamy Soy Soup....97
Red Lentil Soup....98

CASSEROLES AND ONE-DISH MEALS

Mexican Bean Bake....101
2-Bean Skillet Supper....104
Magic Crust Taco Pie....105
Beanchiladas....106
Freezer Bean Burritos....106
Black Bean Burritos....107
Black Bean Taco Pizzas....107
Lizzy's Easy Enchiladas....107
Bean and Rice Burritos....108
Layered Burrito Casserole....108
Colorful Bean Bake....109
Burritos Con Queso....110
Little Lima Bean & Chiles Casseroles....111
Hot and Spicy Black Beans and Rice....111
Mushrooms, Beans and Rice....112
Creamy Vegetable Bean Dish....112
Tamale Pie....115
Sweet and Sour Veggies....114

SIDE DISHES

Fast Refried Beans....123
Instant Refried Bean Mix....123

COMPANY DINNERS

Vegetable Bean Quiche....125
Chicken and Broccoli Quiche....126
Zucchini Quiche....126
Mexican Bean Quiche....126
Oriental Beans and Rice Quiche....127
Oriental Spinach Quiche....127
Linguine with Crab Sauce....127
Cheesey Beans In Crepes....128
Cheese Sauce....128
Mexican Mini Loaves....129
Italian Mini Tofu Loaves....130
Asparagus-Tomato Stir Fry....130

SNACKS, DESSERTS

Refried Beans....123
Super Corn Chips....132
Great Wheat Chips....132
Raspberry Oat Bars....135
No-Wheat Date Cookies....135
Banana Orange Bars....136
Honey Cookies....137
Carob and Soy Brownies....138
Million $$ Bars....138
Spicy Apple Cookies....139
Rich Oatmeal Butterscotch Chip Cookies....139
Peanut Butter Banana Bars....140
Honey Raisin Cookies....140
Peanut Butter Mounds....141
Honey Graham Crackers....141
Carob Chip Mint Cookies....142
Ribbon Cookies....142
Gingerbread Bars....142
Grandma's Best Date Nut Pudding 144
Coconut Oatmeal Cake....145
Grandpa's Carrot Cake....146
Ruth's Honey Sponge Cake....147
Nutty Gingerbread....147
Raisin-Nut Pinto Bean Cake....148
INSTANT MASHED BEANS....155
GRINDING BEAN FLOURS....174
COOKING BEAN FLOUR....3, 79, 173, 180

"Stocking Your Ark" Storage Program

Self-sufficient living is a way of life that involves being practical and thrifty, preparing for the future while attending to today's needs. Learning to store and use basic foods, along with other necessities ("Stocking Your Ark") will help you be self-sustaining in whatever situation you find yourself, whether it be a loss of work, war, civil unrest, famine, tornadoes, hurricanes, earthquakes, fires or floods.

Water is free and easy to store and purify (be sure to store a supply of GSE [Grapefruit Seed Extract] to kill bacteria, viruses, parasites, fungus). **Good quality food will be your most important storage purchase.** The BEST foods are basic foods — beans, grains, and sprouting seeds. They just happen to be the cheapest and easiest foods to store!

Many diseases can be cured or prevented by simply eating an adequate supply of RAW foods. If you can't eat raw food year-round from a garden, take Juice Plus+ (See www.JuicePlusforPrevention.com.) or eat sprouts daily. Canned, bottled or dehydrated fruits and veggies will fill you up and add variety to stored beans and grains, but they take up a lot of space and will not supply the **enzymes** your body needs to be able to heal. If you can't afford to store *everything* all at once, start with at least a 1-month supply of the first six items on this list, adding the other items as your budget permits.

Storage Item	*Adult (Male or Female)*	*Child (to age 6)*
Water	**14 gal.**	**10 gal.**
Water purification drops - (NutriBiotic GSE)	**4 oz.**	**2 oz.**
Wheat	**165 lbs.**	**100 lbs.**
Other Grains (oats, barley, corn, rice, rye)	**80 lbs.**	**50 lbs.**
Sprouting Seeds (to eat and plant)	**60 lbs.**	**30 lbs.**
Legumes (beans, peas, lentils)	**60 lbs.**	**45 lbs.**
Honey (or substitute such as Stevia)	60 lbs.	30 lbs.
Salt	5 lbs.	2 lbs.
Powdered Milk (or alternative)	16-60 lbs.	24-60 lbs.
Fats (olive or canola oil preferred)	2 gal.	1 gal.
Seasoning herbs, spices, mixes (store your favorites)	**	**
Bouillon (for soups and sauces) - enough to flavor...	35 gal. water	15 gal. water
Vegetables & Fruits (dehydrated, bottled, canned)	7-13 serv. per day	5 serv. per day
Whole Food Nutritional Supplements (Juice Plus+***)	4-mo supply	4-mo supply
Yeast (also starters to ferment soy, sourdough, etc.)	4 lbs.	1 lb.
Baking Supplies (leavening agents, carob chips, etc.)	*	*
Cooking equipment (stoves, pans, grinders, etc.)	*	
Fuel (for cooking, lanterns, etc.)	2 wk. supply	2 wk. supply
Medical (first aid, and medications)	*	*
Sanitary Supplies (toilet paper, and personals)	*	*
Personal Care (toothpaste, toothbrushes, dental floss, shampoo, hair spray, deodorant)	*	*
Laundry soap, Clorox bleach, misc. cleaners	*	*
Camping Gear (tents, tarps, backpacks, coats)	*	*
Bedding (sleeping bags, blankets, pillows)	*	*
Scriptures and Legal Documents (waterproofed) individual and family birth certificates, shot records		

* Store on an as-needed basis, depending on how much your family uses, and climate.

** Experiment with recipes to see how much of which seasonings you use.

***Juice Plus+ information and research is available at www.JuicePlusforPrevention.com